With Heart in Mind

BOOKS BY ALAN MORINIS

Climbing Jacob's Ladder: One Man's Journey to Rediscover a Jewish Spiritual Tradition

Everyday Holiness: The Jewish Spiritual Path of Mussar

Every Day, Holy Day: 365 Days of Teachings & Practices from the Jewish Tradition of Mussar

With Heart in Mind

MUSSAR TEACHINGS TO TRANSFORM YOUR LIFE

■ ■ ■ ■ ■ ■ ■

Alan Morinis

TRUMPETER
Boston & London
2014

Trumpeter Books
An imprint of Shambhala Publications, Inc.
Horticultural Hall
300 Massachusetts Avenue
Boston, Massachusetts 02115
www.shambhala.com

9 8 7 6 5 4 3 2 1

First Edition
Printed in the United States of America

⊗ This edition is printed on acid-free paper that meets the
American National Standards Institute Z39.48 Standard.
♻ This book is printed on 30% postconsumer recycled paper.
For more information please visit www.shambhala.com.

Distributed in the United States by Random House, Inc.,
and in Canada by Random House of Canada Ltd

Designed by James D. Skatges

Library of Congress Cataloging-in-Publication Data

Morinis, E. Alan.
With heart in mind: mussar teachings to transform
your life / Alan Morinis.
pages   cm
ISBN 978-1-61180-152-1 (pbk.)
1. Spiritual life—Judaism. 2. Self-actualization (Psychology)
3. Jewish ethics. I. Title.
BM723.M685 2014
296.7—dc23
2013051107

Make for yourself a teacher, acquire for yourself a friend, and judge every person favorably.

—PIRKEI AVOT 1:6

This book is dedicated to the many people who have shared with me the toil and joy of building the Mussar Institute, who have been my teachers and my friends, and who have gifted me with their kindness and their love.

Contents

Contents

Acknowledgments

This book is the result of many minds and hearts applying themselves to the question of what it takes for a human being to develop in the direction of the ideal, stretching back to the anonymous authors of *Pirkei Avot* (Chapters of Root Principles), whose thought provides the core structure for this book.

My dear friends and colleagues at the Mussar Institute, and my students in the Kiyyum program, provided me the opportunity to develop the initial material that formed the foundation for this book. Rabbi Avi Fertig was an invaluable guide and collaborator in the development of some of that course material, and his knowledge and depth of wisdom and understanding show up in so many ways in this rendering.

Rabbi Yechiel Yitzchok and Rebbetzin Shoshana Perr continue to be guiding lights for me in the ways of Mussar, Jewish practice, and life itself. I owe them more than I can say.

Beth Frankl, my able and dear editor, has once again been a steady and supportive presence in bringing this book to completion.

If it reads well, credit is to Beth and to her skilled assistant editor, Ben Gleason.

I am grateful to Jim Levine, my literary agent, for handling so well all the aspects of book creation that fall outside my own focus, so that I could give all my energy and attention to the study and writing that I needed to do.

Bev Spring, my beloved wife, and Julia, Aaron, Leora, and Violet are my immediate family members, who nourish my heart and make my life worth living.

And the older I get and the more I walk my path, the more I know with conviction that there is One Source, to whom I bow in gratitude and lift up my voice in praise.

With Heart in Mind

Introduction

The central concern of Judaism is that you and I accomplish a personal spiritual transformation in our lifetimes. That core intention can be lost in the welter of rituals, festivals, liturgy, and other performative aspects of the tradition. It becomes even less visible when buried under the weight of buildings, institutions, campaigns, and political struggles that are, for some, the face if not the totality of the Jewish world. But the fact remains that, at its core, the driving concern of Judaism is personal spiritual transformation.

How do we know this? For starters, consider the focus of the two holiest days on the ritual calendar—Rosh Hashanah (the Jewish new year) and Yom Kippur (the day of atonement). Yes, there are hundreds of pages of prescribed prayers and many other ritual acts, but the central focus for these two days (as well as the ten days that fall between them) is a personal stock-taking of the things one did or said in the previous year, followed by steps to repair any damage, to set the stage for different behavior in the year to come. The Jerusalem Talmud puts it clearly, "God said, 'Since you all came for judgment before me on Rosh Ha-shanah and you left [the judgment] in peace, I consider it as if you were created as a new being.'"[1]

Redoing ourselves—the project of becoming a new being—is meant to be the central thrust of our lives. And should you think that you are who you are and that change is not possible, over nine hundred years ago, Rambam, also known as Maimonides, affirmed that it is squarely in our own hands to decide who we will be:

> Do not even consider . . . that the Holy Blessed One decrees upon all people at the time of their births whether they will be good or bad. This is not so—every person has the potential to be as righteous as Moses our Teacher, or as wicked as Jeroboam; clever or stupid, merciful or cruel, miserable or noble, or indeed to possess any of the other qualities. Nobody can force you, decree upon you, or lead you into one of the ways, but you should choose a way out of your own free will. . . .[2]

When we realize that the process of transformation is situated at the center of our lives, then all the circumstances that we live with are revisioned as pathways for our growth. The people we relate to, the work we do, where we live, what we eat, the challenges we face, how we respond to those tests, and the rest all appear to be the pieces we are given to work with as we pursue growth. And we do grow. Just by living and having experiences and thinking and learning, we grow. Are you identical to who you were five or ten years ago? It's just not possible, because the very process of living is set up to generate change. Judaism's concern is to make the processes of change deliberate and conscious, and aimed in a particular direction.

Someone raised in the Jewish world in the latter part of the twentieth century is not likely to perceive Judaism as concerned with either personal or spiritual growth. The Jewish world in that period was largely devoted to assimilation, affluence, external show, collective forms, ritual performance, support for the new state of Israel, communal institutions, and recovery from the Holocaust. It made little (if any) room for matters of the interior world of the individual. Despite the fact that the soul in all its dimensions is where we experience life, where we thrive and where we suffer, and where our uniqueness is rooted, the inner life of the individual had been almost entirely eliminated from the Jewish agenda in that recent era.

The price of that neglect has been enormous. Jews continued to seek, but, because a Jewish pathway for inner living was almost impossible to find in the post-Holocaust era, many Jewish seekers wandered into other fields. Many took themselves to Eastern traditions, with their meditation, yoga, and esoteric practices. Others took up self-help disciplines. Quasi-kabbalah slipped into the vacuum. How many Jews became psychologists? And how many of the clients of those psychologists have been Jews? I, too, followed my seeking heart into distant paths, which led to three years in India and a PhD on a topic from the world of Hinduism. How many other Jews simply wandered away from an unsatisfying tradition, with no other destination in mind?

I never felt fully at home in any of the non-Jewish spiritual paths I explored. At a certain point in my life, propelled by a profound sense of lacking direction, I set out to see if I could find guidance for living within the Jewish world. I had a hard time believing that Judaism, despite appearances to the contrary, could have survived for 3,500 years while ignoring the inner life of the individual. My explorations led me to stumble onto

Mussar, a treasure house of practical wisdom and guidance for inner living that has been built up in the Jewish world over the past millennium.

I have been exploring Mussar for the past seventeen years and have written about my encounter with this tradition in my previous books, *Climbing Jacob's Ladder* and *Everyday Holiness*. The main gift that the Mussar tradition makes available to us is a very accurate map of the inner life, along with practices to help us develop in the direction of our ideals.

The proposition that lies at the heart of Mussar is that because life is inherently a process of growing and we have free will, it is within our power and capacity to direct the process of our own change. The wise and compassionate masters who shaped the tradition marked out a step-by-step pathway we can walk to draw closer to the ideals we are capable of manifesting. In so doing, they point us toward two global goals. The highest and best use of a life is to aim toward either *shleimut* (meaning "wholeness") or *kedusha* ("holiness"). These are but two dimensions of the same phenomenon. The more we become living embodiments of our ideals, the more we transition from our partialness (even brokenness) toward becoming more whole, and in wholeness we become vessels for holiness itself. The Mussar masters tell us that this is the open secret that makes sense of the journey of life.

We are not to pursue just any ideals, however. The ideals to which Mussar helps us draw closer come not from our own imaginations or from popular culture or from the philosophers but from the Torah and its interpretations (which are also part of the Torah). The Torah articulates stunning ideals for what a human being can be. In the five Books of Moses, the word *kindness* (*chesed*) appears 248 times. Generosity, compassion, grace, patience, and love are all held up as divine qualities we are meant to embody in our own lives. And Mussar gives us the tools to help us internalize those qualities, and so to change, and so to become more whole and more holy.

Because the Torah plays a very central role in this book and to ensure that there is no misunderstanding, I want to clarify what I am referring to when I say "Torah."

Most familiarly, "Torah" refers to the five Books of Moses, the scroll of the law that starts with the Book of Genesis and the creation of the world and ends with Moses's lessons delivered as the people stand poised to enter the Promised Land without him. These five books are the core of the written Torah, but there is more. Also included in the written Torah are the books of the prophets (Isaiah, Ezekiel, Jeremiah, and so on) and the books known as the writings (Proverbs, Psalms, Ecclesiastes, etc.).

Then there is the oral Torah, as distinct from the written Torah. In the centuries after the written Torah was received, the rabbis and sages probed to understand what the five Books of Moses, the prophets, and writings had to say. Sometimes they sought deep and esoteric meaning and sometimes just how to define certain words or understand the simple meaning of a law or how and when it applied. The rabbinic code was first recorded in the Mishnah (200 C.E.), and the Mishnah was later expanded upon and incorporated into the Talmud (500 C.E.). This is the oral Torah.

And there is even more. What I am really talking about when I say "Torah" is the wisdom of all sorts that has been accumulated within the Jewish tradition. The word *Torah* has the simple meaning "teaching" or "law" and is derived from a linguistic root used in archery to refer to shooting an arrow to hit a target. The writings and thought of Torah are an arrow aimed at Truth. Jewish tradition has always taught that Torah provides the blueprint for human experience, and so when we understand what the Torah teaches and bring its lessons into our lives, we acquire for ourselves the truth it contains.

For centuries, Jews have studied Torah, some to learn the Torah's lessons and some to go beyond learning to what the rabbis have called "acquiring" Torah. Learning Torah and acquiring Torah are not synonymous. Learning Torah means studying the stories and concepts of the Torah in order to arrive at a full understanding of what they mean and entail. But many sources tell us that we should not let what we learn remain intellectual concepts, mere information. Grasping the definition of *humility* is not the same as being humble, for example. Being able to cite all the reasons that one should trust God is not necessarily going to ease the anxious heart into tranquility.

This book is devoted to helping you bring the wisdom and goodness of Torah into your life. Had the rabbis wanted us to make learning Torah the goal, they would have said just that. When they direct us to *acquire* Torah, they are informing us that there is a stage beyond learning where the truths we have learned get worked into the very core of our being, into our hearts, so that truth will be the guiding light of our thoughts, feelings, words, and deeds.[3]

Approaching Torah with the heart in mind means setting ourselves not just to learn but also to internalize the Torah's ideals. When that happens, it brings about a genuine transformation of the inner self, giving rise to inspiration, a passionate and joyful infusion that effects change in every aspect of being, and hence daily life.

The Mussar teachers focused on the practical steps we can take to internalize the teachings of the Torah for the sake of this personal transformation. A recent Mussar master, Rabbi Elya Lopian,[4] actually defined Mussar as "making the heart feel what the intellect understands." Making the heart feel what the mind knows requires learning and then another step beyond. It requires a foray into the territory of *acquiring* the wisdom of Torah and making it your own. This step to acquire the Torah's truths is the focus of this book. My goal here is to help you open doorways through which new spiritual ideas can come to you, ideas that you will not just learn but that you will acquire, so they take root in the inner reaches of your heart to become part of the essence of who you are.

Usually, we acquire things by exchanging something of value in return. What can you offer to acquire Torah? The only thing that will effect this exchange is your effort. You have to "toil in Torah" to get what Torah has to offer. Because acquiring Torah means instilling its teachings in the heart and not just the mind, acquiring Torah is achieved through a variety of practices that include but then go beyond the realm of learning.

Everything we learn and all the ideals we hold are mere concepts until we do the practices that cause those notions to become woven into the very fabric of our being, to become part of our very selves. The Mussar masters recognized that change comes about only as a result of experiences generated through practice.

Practice is therefore central to that act of acquiring Torah. We can learn facts from Torah, and many people would easily recognize phrases from the Bible—like "Let my people go" or "Love your neighbor as yourself"—but the acquisition of Torah takes effect when what we learn is transformed through practice from an intellectual concept into *da'at* or *da'as*—intimate, internalized knowledge. Rabbi Avi Fertig writes,

> Acquiring Torah [*kinyan*] is a function of *da'as*. Intimate knowledge is knowledge that connects every part of my being. Man is composed of several dualisms: body and

soul, mind and emotions, and *seichel* [intellect] and *middos* [character]. When Torah penetrates our entire being, when not just our *seichel* . . . , [this is the *acquisition* of Torah].[5]

Over the centuries, wise and compassionate Jewish teachers have identified effective methods we can practice to bring Torah into our innermost being. A traditional guide to such practices can be found in a book of pithy aphorisms and wisdom known as *Pirkei Avot* (often translated as *Chapters of the Fathers* but better rendered *Chapters of Root Principles*) that is part of the Mishnah and so dates from about 200 C.E. Chapter 6 of *Pirkei Avot* was added somewhat later but is now considered an integral part of the book. That chapter contains a teaching (6:6) that lists forty-eight methods through which one can acquire Torah. These methods are very practical, accessible, and universal and are as effective for instilling truth in the heart of people like you and me today as they were hundreds of years ago when they were codified in *Pirkei Avot*.

The teaching reads as follows:

Torah is greater than the priesthood or sovereignty, for sovereignty is acquired with thirty virtues, the priesthood with twenty-four, and Torah is acquired with forty-eight qualities.

These are: study, listening, verbalizing, comprehension of the heart, awe/fear, humility, joy, purity, serving the sages, companionship with one's contemporaries, debating with one's students, tranquility, study of the scriptures, study of the Mishnah, minimizing engagement in business, minimizing socialization, minimizing

pleasure, minimizing sleep, minimizing talk, minimizing gaiety, slowness to anger, good heartedness, faith in
the sages, acceptance of suffering, knowing one's place,
satisfaction with one's lot, qualifying one's words, not
taking credit for oneself, likableness, love of God, love of
humanity, love of charity, love of justice, love of rebuke,
fleeing from honor, lack of arrogance in learning, reluctance to hand down rulings, participating in the burden
of one's fellow, judging him to the side of merit, correct-
ing him, bringing him to a peaceful resolution [of his
disputes], deliberation in study, asking and answering,
listening and illuminating, learning in order to teach,
learning in order to observe, wising one's teacher, exact-
ness in conveying a teaching, and saying something in
the name of its speaker. Thus we have learned: One who
says something in the name of its speaker brings redemption to the world, as is stated (Esther 2:22), "And Esther
told the king in the name of Mordechai."

What we have here is a curriculum of spiritual qualities that
have been not only revered but also practiced by Jewish spiritual
seekers throughout the millennia. It also provides the table of
contents for this book, which will explore all forty-eight methods for bringing about the inner transformation that is called
acquiring Torah. And because this far-reaching transformation
of self is more than an intellectual exercise, each chapter explains one of the transformative methods listed in the verse in
Pirkei Avot and also provides a practice you can do to enact that
method so that its essence will become embedded in your heart.
 The text itself identifies that there are forty-eight methods
for acquiring Torah, but, as anyone who knows something about
the study of Jewish text might expect, there is more than one

way in which the qualities and attributes given in *Pirkei Avot* 6:6 have been broken down into a list of forty-eight. In fact, if you count them up one by one, there appear to be fifty-one individual items! From the sixteenth century until more recently, commentators have argued for various listings that total forty-eight. Working with colleagues, I have compared several different versions of the list to come up with the one I present here. It is the closest to a consensus version we could devise.

The approach is holistic, and so some of the forty-eight methods are cognitive, like deliberation in study and asking and answering. Others are social, including close association with colleagues, serving scholars, and discussing matters with students. Some are behavioral, like moderation in conversation, moderation in pleasure, and the like. There are emotions, including love directed in several ways. Many are traits of character, like humility and cheerfulness, patience, and a good heart.

It may be daunting to think of mastering forty-eight separate and diverse methods in order to taste the fruit of this practice, and, in fact, commenting on the verse from *Pirkei Avot* that is our guide, the great Jewish sage of the eighteenth century, the Vilna Gaon, assures us that no one can master all forty-eight pathways. Each individual is capable of mastering only several of these methods. Since it is impossible for one person to perfect himself or herself in all forty-eight ways, the Vilna Gaon gives us a staff to lean on as we walk this path. Of all the forty-eight, one method is the most essential: *ohev et habriyot*—to love your fellow humans.

This guideline reveals a central truth about Jewish spiritual practice—it doesn't ask us to retreat from the ordinary realms of life and to avoid the messy world of people and relationships. Rather, it identifies noisy and complicated everyday life as the ideal place to work at spiritual growth. Nowhere are we tested as we are by our interactions with other people. When you set out to love other people, as the Vilna Gaon[6] directs, you are bound to find every spiritual obstacle that lurks within you popping up to challenge your aspirations. You try to be loving and find you are impatient. You try to be loving, and instead you are judgmental. You try to be loving, and what comes out is your own desires. Whatever qualities you have in you that have some potential to grow and become more whole will be thrust to the fore by the trials of trying to love others. Nothing brings your personal spiritual curriculum into high relief as does the effort to love other people.

Setting yourself to loving other people creates an opportunity to deal with the aspects of your inner self that are less than whole. Those incomplete traits define your personal spiritual curriculum. If you do the work to support that growth, you will make progress toward acquiring the inner way of being that the Torah tells us is ideal and that the Mussar masters call whole and holy. Then you'll be truly ready to love. And if you don't do that work, the sad and inevitable fact is that you will keep getting the same life tests over and over again, until you either wake up to accomplishing the growth that has been assigned to you, or you learn your lessons the hard way, by means of bitter experience.

It is entirely possible that all the learning and practice you have done throughout your life has prepared you for this very moment, and that the excursion we will now make into processes to acquire Torah will be the final .1 percent that will ignite a total transformation of your soul. Or it may be that the changes you will see happening will be smaller and more incremental. It doesn't really matter how far you get. The most important thing is that you point your feet in the right direction on the path that leads up the holy mountain, and that you go.

HOW TO USE THIS BOOK

Study

Each of the forty-eight methods that we will explore in this book is developed by means of a lesson based on traditional concepts. The interpretive lesson is needed because even if the methods outlined here seem entirely familiar and obvious to you, in most cases, there is a specifically Jewish slant that is not intuitive and needs to be brought out in order to gain the insights of Jewish wisdom in that area.

For example, no one reading this book is likely to ask for a definition of terms like *joy* or *humility,* but, in fact, the Jewish understanding of these inner states is far removed from their English synonyms of *happiness* and *meekness.* How much more is that the case when we encounter specifically Jewish spiritual practices, like "serving the sages" and "reluctance to hand down decisions." Each chapter offers insight into the spiritual method brought into focus there.

The lessons are my own interpretations based in traditional sources. I have drawn much from a work called *Midrash Shmuel,* a sixteenth-century commentary on *Pirkei Avot* written by Rabbi Shmuel d'Ouzida of Venice. Many of the lessons were road tested in a program of the Mussar Institute in which students focused on one lesson per day during the forty-nine-day period between Passover and Shavuot (the time of the counting of the Omer), as was done in the nineteenth-century Mussar yeshiva of Rabbi Simcha Zissel Ziv.[7] I had the help of my friend and colleague Rabbi Avi Fertig to develop some of that course material. In the end, the lessons are my own synthesis of the Mussar wisdom that has come to me from many sources, representing to the best of my ability the insights and guidance that have developed in this 1,100-year-old Jewish spiritual tradition.

Practice

Once a concept is clarified, it can be "acquired" only by means of practice, and with that goal in mind, I provide a Mussar practice for each of the forty-eight methods we explore here. Practice is necessary because it is sure that there will be very little tangible impact in your life if all you get from the concept of "loving your fellow humans" or "purity" is a clarification of what the term means and that idea remains lodged between your ears.

In bringing practice into every one of the subjects we will soon study together, I am being true to the tradition into which I have set my own spiritual roots. One of the things that drew me to Mussar in the beginning and that remains true as I continue to explore its ancient pathways is that it puts great store in personal spiritual practice. Practice is what transforms truthful ideas into living truths.

When Rabbi Shlomo Wolbe, another great twentieth-century Mussar teacher, defined Mussar, he called it "building your interior world." He came to the same conclusion as Rav Elya Lopian: "Building" happens not through expanding the number of notations in your mental files but through experiential practice.

I have often quoted one of my early Mussar teachers, Rabbi Moshe Broide, who once said to me succinctly, "You don't study Mussar. You *do* Mussar." And so, too, with the "acquisition of Torah," that is our focus here. There is an element of learning that needs to be done to gain understanding, but we are not meant to stop with mere conceptual understanding. The internalization and transformative impact—the acquisition that is the goal—happen through actually engaging in the practices like those I describe and assign.

Schedule

The ideal way to use this book is to read one chapter per week, doing the practice that comes in that chapter for that entire week. Mussar practice generally follows that pattern—you adopt a single focus for one week, then move on to the next focus in the following week, and so on. You'll find that schedule easy to keep if you fix a certain time in the week when you read the new chapter and begin the practice that you will continue to do all seven days of that week.

Reading one chapter and then doing its practice for a week will have a cumulative effect—you will see for yourself that seven days practicing one method has a remarkable capacity to stamp that quality on your heart. As you go from method to method, you'll find that the previous methods are not really left behind. They become part of who you are and part of what you bring to the next practices.

If you follow this pattern of reading and practice, it will take you almost a year to complete this book. By that point, you will have gained many new insights into yourself, much awareness of the spiritual curriculum that is your soul-work in this life, and knowledge of practices that will help instill precious qualities in your heart. You will have made strides in the direction of the transformation that is called acquiring Torah, and you will know with clarity what steps to take next on that journey.

Finally . . . there is one other way to use this book: Dip into it as needed. The Mussar masters understood that the challenges and tests that show up in every life are important to our spiritual growth. The forty-eight topics explored in this book cover a lot of the territories where those tests might well come your way. My hope and my prayer are that the wisdom accumulated in the Mussar tradition that I am sharing here will be a source of light and guidance to you in times of challenge, when the choices you make have a real impact on the soul you are.

MY PRAYER

This book is a handbook for learning and practice based in a traditional Jewish source that aims to open doorways through which new spiritual ideas can come—ideas that will not just be learned but will also take root in the depths of your inner being, there to bring about an alchemical change of heart.

If you use it diligently, you will find yourself echoing previous generations of students who have reflected on their acquisition of Torah by saying that they simply are not the same person they used to be, students like the one who sent me a note that reported the following:

> My sister is very difficult. She is deeply grieving my mother's passing, isn't feeling well, and her car broke down. She was going to miss our weekly family dinner, so I arranged to pick her up (about a 45-minute drive each way) and have my brother bring her home. We didn't fight because I didn't become triggered. From some mysterious place there welled up in me compassion and the desire to treat her the way I would want to be treated. Honestly, I hardly recognized myself. Somehow, I wanted to and felt I could help her bear her burden. These are the accumulating traces of Mussar.

My prayer is that you will find in *With Heart in Mind* an introduction to the venerable insights and methodologies that generations of seekers have found valuable in their pursuit of a heart of wisdom, and that it will provide guidance to direct your footsteps along those transformative paths, so that you will become more whole and holy and a gift and blessing to yourself, those around you, and our world.

תלמוד

[1]

Study

Talmud

These are the things for which a person enjoys the dividends in
this world while the principal remains to enjoy in the world to
come. They are: honoring parents, deeds of lovingkindness and
making peace between one person and another. But the study
of the Torah is equal to them all.

—*Shabbat* 127A

THE FIRST METHOD by which to acquire Torah is the quint-
essentially Jewish spiritual practice of "study." We learn
two things from the fact that the rabbis positioned study as the
first of the forty-eight methods through which we acquire
Torah.

First, this underlines the point made earlier that "acquiring
Torah" should not be confused with "learning Torah." Learning Torah is a method, while acquiring Torah is a goal. Learning
Torah involves study, while acquiring Torah involves a personal
transformation.

The second reason study is given pride of place is the importance Jewish tradition has always given to the study of texts and

the quest for knowledge. For thousands of years, the study of biblical, Talmudic, and rabbinic writings has been the central Jewish practice for personal refinement and spiritual elevation. Study has occupied the highest tier on the scale of values, exceeding the combined worth of such praiseworthy deeds as honoring your parents, being kind, creating peace, and the like. It is said that God weeps over the person who could have occupied himself or herself with Torah study but neglected to do so.[1]

Right in the Bible itself the command is given, "Teach [these words] to your children, talk about them when you sit at home and when you walk along the road, when you lie down and when you get up,"[2] instructions to engage in study that have been incorporated into the daily liturgy.

Through Torah study we learn right from wrong, starting with the Ten Commandments. We also learn morality, good from bad. Engagement with peers and teachers is praised because it sharpens the intellect. But the rabbinic tradition tells us that Torah study is that and more. The Torah predates history and is actually the blueprint for the creation of the universe, and so we study Torah not only to learn the stories and the laws but also to delve into the foundations of all existence and to discover what we can of the nature of God. Century upon century, Jews have been passionately engaged with study and learning, singly, in pairs, and in groups; and whether explicitly or implicitly, the subject of study has always been the nature of the holy within this world.

Because the Torah is studied, there is always the danger that what is learned will be nothing more than information, a mere expansion of a conceptual inventory. Rabbinic writings inveigh against this approach to study starting with verse 1:2 from the Song of Songs, which says, "O, let him kiss me with the kisses of his mouth." They offer an allegorical interpretation that this verse is not about a lover but about God.[3] The seeker yearns for the kiss of the divine. That kiss takes place through the medium of Torah study, and it is a kiss that is always available.

Thus the aim of study is not only to learn rules of behavior and about the holy and the ways of the universe, and also about God, but also through the act of study to become directly intimate with the divine. Rabbi Chaim of Volozhin (1749–1821), the founder of the modern yeshiva, describes the mystical intimacy that comes from study: "For the occupation and study themselves involve communion with the will and the word of the Blessed One, and the Blessed One and His will and His Word are all one."[4] Through study we encounter the word, and the word reveals the will of God. God is present in the word and the will, and so through this activity a person experiences mystical intimacy with the One.

No wonder, then, that Torah study is described as pure pleasure. The Chazon Ish (1878–1953), a recent sage, wrote,

> No pleasure in this world can equal that of diligent Torah study. Sweet experiences can impart a sense of pleasure to a person's body, and to all his limbs in a limited sense. But this pleasure can never compete with the inestimable pleasure of toiling for the wisdom of Torah, in which a person's soul is lifted above; where it absorbs pleasure from the glow of elevated wisdom.[5]

All this comes from Torah study. But hearkening back to the introduction to this book, *Torah* is defined more broadly than as a set of texts, and so the study of Torah involves more than poring over books. Our study is not meant to be restricted to the printed word. In *Pirkei Avot* 4:1 the question is asked, "Who is wise?" And the answer is given, "One who learns from everyone." The Hebrew says, *mi'kol adam,* which can indeed mean "from everyone," and yet the nineteenth-century Mussar teacher Rabbi Simcha Zissel Ziv preferred to interpret this phrase to mean learning "from the *entire* person," which the Hebrew permits.[6]

He draws our attention to the way, for example, the clothing designer notices your suit but pays little attention to whether you are kind. The thief does not see your hat or your shoes but only your wallet. The dog lover sees every detail of the dog but barely perceives the owner. Our tendency is to focus only where we already have an interest, and so we miss out on learning as much from others as we could. The truly wise person is open to learning from every possible aspect of every situation and every person he or she encounters.

Indeed, the Jewish term for a learned person is not a *chacham,* a wise one, but a *talmid chacham,* which literally translates to "a wise student." The truly wise individual is not one who has achieved wisdom but rather one who is constantly seeking learning, ever studying more—including by observing and reflecting on what can be learned from other people—for that has become his or her mode of living, and the thirst is strong.

The rabbis attribute a power to Torah study, but, like all forms of power, it can be put to positive or negative uses. Which of these is true for us depends on our personal character, and here the practice of Mussar comes into the picture. The Vilna Gaon[7] notes that Torah study is compared to rain,[8] and from that he draws a lesson:

> Do not assume that Torah study guarantees that the one who pursues it will become a refined person. The rain comes to the entire land equally but its effect depends on

the recipient. If the land was sowed with wheat, it will sprout wheat. If it was sowed with a poisonous plant, it will sprout a poisonous plant. So too the Torah; if his heart is good, his reverence will become greater. If his heart is bad, he will fail all the more so when pondering it and the resentment within his heart will grow.

If study were all it took to bring about personal transformation, we could stop our work right here. But the rabbis provide us with forty-seven additional practices toward this goal, and here we learn why. Additional practices are needed to help us elevate our character traits (*middot*) and to improve our behavior, so that the seeds that flourish in us through Torah study will produce nothing but healthy, nourishing fruit.

PRACTICE

Since we are enjoined to "learn from everyone," and in light of the Alter of Kelm's beautiful interpretation that we should set ourselves to learning from the *entire* person, your practice is to place a piece of paper or a small notebook in your pocket or bag and to write down at least one thing you can learn from every person you meet every day of this period, without exception.

שמיעת האוזן

[2]

Attentive Listening

Shmiat ha'Ozen

A great and powerful wind tore the mountains apart and shattered the rocks before the Lord, but the Lord was not in the wind. After the wind there was an earthquake, but the Lord was not in the earthquake. After the earthquake came a fire, but the Lord was not in the fire. And after the fire came a gentle whisper. When Elijah heard it, he pulled his cloak over his face and went out and stood at the mouth of the cave.

—I KINGS 19:11–13

RABBI YISRAEL SALANTER (1810–83) started the Mussar movement in Lithuania in the mid-nineteenth century. After fifteen years leading the movement, he moved to Memel, in what was then Prussia. Ironically, we are fortunate that he relocated so far from his students, because he wrote them letters that have been preserved and that provide us with almost the only record we have of his thoughts on spiritual self-improvement.[1]

In the very first of these letters, he admonishes his students because they had not followed through with his plan to introduce the study of Mussar to the community. He writes to them,

"My primary aspiration that I desire [for you to accomplish] is a matter that I have consistently presented before you. [I expected that you would] set your hearts upon them [i.e., my instructions] and deeply contemplate them. In truth, have I uttered any words? It almost seems that the moment my words enter your ears—in the very next moment—they become nonexistent. My words entered one ear and exited the other."

It's not an unfamiliar criticism. So often words are spoken that are not heard, or not heard deeply or completely enough. The next quality one who would acquire Torah needs to develop is "a listening ear," *shmiat ha'ozen* in Hebrew. The word *shmiat* comes from the root *shma,* to hear or listen. *Ozen* is the Hebrew word for ear. Therefore, this quality is, literally, "a listening ear," or, we might say, attentive listening.

Hearing is a physiological and involuntary act; listening is something different. Listening means inclining the mind so as to register in consciousness what the sound waves are conveying through the ear. It means digging in to unpack the meaning within the sounds. Being an attentive listener requires that and more. So often, the message is not only in the meaning of the words but in the emotion or tone in which they are said or the body language of the person speaking, as well. An attentive listener pays attention and picks up on all of it.

We learn about a listening ear from a story told about Rabbi Yosef Dov Soloveitchik (1820–92). A man approached the rabbi to ask if it would be permissible to fulfill the obligation of drinking four glasses at the ritual Passover seder with milk instead of the usual wine. The rabbi asked the man if he was considering making that switch because he was ill. No, the man told him, his health was not the issue. Wine was just more expensive than he could afford.

The rabbi then gave the man twenty-five rubles. After the

man left, the rabbi's wife asked why he had given the man so much when two or three rubles would have been enough to buy wine. The rabbi said, "If that man was thinking of drinking milk at the seder, not only did he not have enough money for wine, he didn't have enough money for meat or other necessities of the seder, either."

What was the question? Could milk be used instead of wine for the ritual? Was that what R' Yosef Dov heard? No—because he really listened, he was able to hear so much more.

Listening is given a very special place in Jewish practice. The primary affirmation and declaration of faith in one God—the *Shema*—is recited morning and evening in the liturgy: "Hear O Israel, the Lord is our God, the Lord is One."[2] Jewish practice calls for real concentration when reciting the *Shema,* and so people commonly close their eyes or cover them with their hand while reciting this line to eliminate distraction and to facilitate deep concentration.

Why the emphasis on concentration? Because it is entirely possible (and maybe too common) to recite this line of prayer in the most rote and perfunctory way. But that's to miss the point. It requires a strong inner attunement to turn this oral statement into a conscious and effective declaration. The "hearing" I am called to perform is a sincere inner affirmation that there is but one divine source and power in all the universe. When I enter my consciousness into that declaration, I experience an accurate assessment of the truth of my place in the world. My inner being is suffused with acceptance of the "yoke of heaven," the implications of the words I just said and deeply heard.

Listening attentively is how we catch all that is sent our way from others, whether pearls of wisdom, or rebuke, or just good information. This is something we would all agree is important, but it is not an easy thing to do. Ears alone do not guarantee that one is listening, and it may take work to become an attentive listener.

The first step toward developing this quality is to become aware of what might be keeping you from paying close attention to what you hear from your teachers, whether those who teach at the front of a classroom or those you encounter on the street and in the supermarket. We want to become aware of the factors that cause us to have *arel ozen* (uncircumcised ears)—"Behold, their ears are uncircumcised; they cannot listen."[3]

Perhaps it is simply a lack of concentration—the teacher is there, but where are you? Maybe somewhere else in your own mind.

A lack of humility can obstruct your ears. It's well recognized (and will show up in chapter 35) that arrogance is a huge obstacle to listening to what others have to say.[4]

It could be a lack of contemplation. To really grasp a lesson, the message must be contemplated in light of our personal lives.

As an example of the need to contemplate and not just act on what we have heard, Rav Yechezkiel Levenstein (1895–1974), a revered Mussar supervisor of the Ponevezh Yeshiva, once remarked, "If immediately after listening to my Mussar talk someone prays with more enthusiasm, he didn't understand the talk and *never* will understand it!"[5] He meant that to truly perceive his message, one must not just hear it but contemplate it deeply. If his words result in a quick burst of emotional energy, the message of the talk will be lost to the student forever. He is not likely ever to contemplate the message because he thinks the desired result has already occurred, and therefore he will miss the essential message that is personally relevant to his situation.

Truly listening does not mean just having information pass through the ears and into the brain; it means to *hear* all of the message.

PRACTICE

Everyone has something to teach you. It could be your formal teachers or maybe the FedEx driver or the café waitress. Everyone you meet is a holy soul, a *neshama,* imbued with elements of wisdom of his or her own. If you listen. If you incline your ear.

The usual translation of *shmiat ha'ozen* is to be a careful listener. To be "careful" is to be attentive but also "full of care." Your practice today is to listen to what others say to you in a more acute fashion. Follow the example of Rabbi Yosef Dov Soloveitchik and ask yourself, What is he or she *really* saying?

Whether in a formal setting of learning or by being attentive to everyone you meet along your way, incline your ear with depth and attention to hear the deeper messages in what people express to you. The more you do this, the better you will get to be at doing it.

עריכת שפתים

3

Orderly Speech

Arichat Sefatayim

Seven characteristics typify the clod, and seven the wise
person: Wise people do not speak in the presence of those who
are wiser than they are; They do not interrupt their friend's
words; They do not reply in haste. They ask what is relevant,
they answer to the point; they reply to questions in orderly se-
quence; of what they have not heard, they say, "I have not
heard." They admit to the truth. The opposite of these typify
the clod.

—PIRKEI AVOT 5:9

THE ABILITY to utter intelligible speech is not only a distinctive characteristic of the human species, it is truly a
wonder. My vocal cords make a series of sounds that create vibrations in the air that enter your ears and are transmitted to
your brain, where they are converted back into the meaning that
originated in my brain. How wondrous is that!

Classical Jewish thought divides the world into the following domains:

- *domeim* (silent; inanimate)
- *tzomeiach* (growing; plants)
- *chai* (living; animals)
- *medaber* (speaking; people)

In this hierarchy, the lowest form of existence is silent, while speaking is the symbol of the highest category, the human. It is the capacity to speak that differentiates the human from all other categories of creation.

When the Torah was translated into Aramaic,[1] the translator, Onkelos, rendered the end of the verse "The Lord God formed Adam from the dust of the ground and breathed into his nostrils the breath of life, and Adam became *a living soul*"[2] as "Adam became *a speaking spirit*."[3] (Emphasis is mine.) Rabbi Chaim of Volozhin explains that Onkelos translated "living soul" as "speaking spirit" because the power of speech is located in a dimension of the soul called the *ruach* and the *ruach* is seated in the heart, the source and center of our lives.[4] The words we speak are the outward expression of who we are at heart. In turn, the words we speak affect our hearts.

From the moment of our creation, we were formed to be communicative beings. It's our speaking soul that defines our humanity. *That* we speak establishes us as human, but *how* we speak defines the kind of human being we happen to be. Speech is not just a power; it is a responsibility. Indeed, we read in Proverbs 18:21, "Death and life are in the power of the tongue."

Our current method is called *arichat sefatayim* in Hebrew, which literally means "arranged lips." Because words are so powerful, we must be sure they are properly arranged so that they are put to positive rather than negative effect. *Pirkei Avot* 5:9, quoted in the chapter epigraph, gives us the seven characteristics of a wise person, and you can see that they are all matters of how a person speaks. When a person speaks in opposite ways, that signifies that he or she is a clod or boor.

Rabbi Avraham Yitzchok Kook (1865–1935), the first Ashkenazi chief rabbi of Israel, reflects on how a person on the spiritual path comes increasingly to see the importance of speech:

> As the soul is elevated, we become acutely aware of the tremendous power that lies in our faculty of speech. We recognize clearly the tremendous significance of each utterance; the value of our prayers and blessings, the value of our Torah study and of all of our discourse. We learn to perceive the overall impact of speech. We sense the change and great stirring of the world that comes about through speech.[5]

The positive potential of speech is revealed in Jewish thought in the most dramatic way. The very creation of the world and everything that is in it was accomplished by means of words alone. "And God *said,* 'Let there be light' and there was light."[6] Other divine utterances follow, each one causing the creation of an important dimension of our world.[7] Psalms 33:6 describes, "Through the word of God, the heavens were made; and through the breath of His mouth, all of their hosts."

Speech has that much power to be creative. In Hebrew, the word *davar* means both "word" and "thing," teaching us that something that is spoken brings an actual reality into existence. According to Rabbeinu Yonah of Gerona (1180–1263), when you are careful about what words you speak, you sanctify yourself like a holy vessel used in the temple service.[8] A holy vessel is suitable only for the highest purpose, and so it is with our mouths. If all your words are for an elevated purpose, then your mouth is as holy as the temple vessels.

The opposite is true of negative speech (*lashon ha'ra*), which is so reviled in Jewish thought that it is said to be a form of murder, and not just that, murder of three people—the one who utters the negative words, the one about whom they are spoken, and the one who hears them.[9] The laws of negative speech are many, but they all boil down to one principle: Do no harm with your speech.

The twentieth-century sage the Chafetz Chaim codified the laws of speech.[10] Among the sources he drew on is verse 21:23 from Proverbs, which says, "One who guards his mouth and tongue, guards his *nefesh*-soul from troubles." We all know from experience how much grief can come from an ill-considered word. It actually happened that when the police confronted two gangsters and demanded that one hand over his gun, the other told the one with the gun, "Let him have it." The armed gangster then shot the policeman. In court, the accomplice pleaded innocent because he said he meant for his partner to hand over his gun, not to shoot, both valid interpretations of "let him have it."

The Chafetz Chaim takes the tribulations that follow from wrong speech to another level, however. He agrees that speaking is the essential and defining feature of the human soul, and so words uttered in harmful ways impair the soul in its essential quality. The impact is felt not just in life, however, but on the soul itself, and that impact will last for all eternity and is the source of the soul's ultimate tribulation.[11]

Psalms 34:13 therefore declares, "Who is the person who desires life, who loves days of seeing good? Guard your tongue from evil and your lips from speaking deceit." The impact of our speech is felt in our days in this world and in the days of all eternity.

PRACTICE

The act of verbalization has power. It clarifies ideas and concretizes concepts, turning them from fuzzy mental notions into a reality in the world. When the Mishnah says that your lips are to be orderly, that means that you should take care that what comes out of your mouth lines up with your values and ideals.

In this period, pay special attention to everything that comes out of your mouth and assay every sentence to ensure that it carries into reality only your highest aspirations.

בינת הלב

[4]

Understanding of the Heart

Binat ha'Lev

I have given you a wise and understanding heart.

—I KINGS 3:12

PSYCHOLOGISTS ACCEPT that there is more than one kind of intelligence. The intellect can be measured on the scale of the IQ, but that is not the only form of intelligence with which we are equipped. Psychological theories tend to be concerned only with the mind, so they don't include the type of understanding (*binah*) that comes directly through the heart (*lev*). From a spiritual perspective, understanding of the heart is more important than that of the mind, because the heart is the organ through which we can grasp the most profound and eternal matters, from love to God.

This method for acquiring Torah is *binat ha'lev*, "understanding of the heart."[1] The translation here is important. This is not the same as "an understanding heart," which is outwardly focused and could be called empathy. It is rather "understanding *of* the heart," which is inwardly focused and reflects spiritual intelligence, or what might otherwise be called wisdom.

In Mussar thought, the heart is more than the emotional center. It is the core and essence of the human being. It is the seat of the personality, the center of emotion, attitudes, values, and intellect and the place within us where we make contact with God. The heart is where we experience life in all its ups and downs, ins and outs, as the *midrash* points out in listing the many features of the human heart that are cited in the Torah, "The heart speaks, hears, walks, falls, stands, rejoices, cries, envies, breaks, strives, desires, grows faint, fears, is comforted, repents, hardens, melts, rends, is deceived" and more.[2] The Hebrew word for heart shows up no fewer than 850 times in scripture.

The kind of understanding that we do within our hearts is very valued in Jewish thought. God comes to King Solomon in a dream and says, "Ask for what you want and I will give it to you."[3] Solomon could have asked for anything: wealth, power, or honor. But instead he asked for understanding of the heart. God granted this wish and gave Solomon the inner capacity for understanding he sought. What followed was that he became known as the wisest of men.[4] And he also got all the things he did not ask for, including riches, power, and honor.

From that fragment of the story, you might be tempted to think that understanding of the heart can only be attained as a gift from God, but that is not so. Solomon was already king of Israel when he asked for understanding of the heart. He had worked hard to merit the gift he received.

In the *Amidah,* the silent prayers that are repeated three times daily, the fourth of the nineteen prayers is *"Atah chonen l'adam da'at, u'melamed le'enosh binah"*—"You grant to the person knowledge and teach the human being understanding."

The use of the verb "teach" in this prayer underlines that *binah* is not a free gift but is an inner quality that needs to be learned and earned. Knowledge (*da'at*) can be freely granted, but the quality of understanding of the heart comes to us by means of our efforts. Rabbi Yerucham Levovitz (1873–1936), the revered Mussar supervisor of the Mir Yeshiva in prewar Poland, explains that only when we work hard to grasp understanding will an idea we have learned connect with our hearts and penetrate to the level of our deepest selves.[5]

There is a story about the Vilna Gaon that tells of him being approached by a heavenly emissary who offered to reveal to him many secrets of Torah and heaven:[6]

> The angelic messenger pressed him greatly, but he did not look upon the angel's great countenance. He answered and told him, "I do not want my grasp of God's Torah to come through any intermediary; my eyes are raised only to Him. That which God wishes to reveal to me and give me as my portion in His Torah He will give to me in wisdom for the work I have done with all of my energy. From His mouth comes intellect and comprehension, when He gives me a heart to understand."

In the face of the opportunity to come to know precious and as yet unrevealed truths, the Gaon turned down the offer. He didn't want to learn or understand anything that he did not work to achieve. He sought understanding of the heart that was earned through his own effort.

The Vilna Gaon understood the role of Mussar in achieving heart-based wisdom. A letter to his wife is preserved, in which he wrote, "You will find among my books a number of Yiddish Mussar books. The children should read them constantly especially on the holy Shabbos, when Mussar books are the only thing that they should read. In fact you should constantly guide them with Mussar books."[7] He is often quoted as saying that improving one's soul-traits is the most important activity a person can engage in.

Mussar learning and practice help develop understanding of the heart. That connection is established in the very first chapter of the book of Proverbs, verse 1:2, where King Solomon explains that he is providing these proverbs in order that the reader will come "to know wisdom and Mussar and to apprehend words of understanding [*binah*]."

Your heart comes equipped with an innate capacity to be understanding, and you would be a person of great wisdom, except that something gets in the way. What obstructs your access to your own heart's wisdom is the condition the Mussar teachers call *timtum ha'lev*—an obstructed or stopped-up heart. The heart becomes spiritually blocked with the residues of the inner qualities (*middot,* or "soul-traits") that are out of balance. These qualities are where a person has the potential to grow.

At every moment, every person has some *middot* that are partial or stunted or extreme, and that set of traits makes up that individual's personal spiritual curriculum. Someone's habit of being arrogant, or greedy, or envious serves to block his or her heart from being understanding and divert it toward being grasping and self-interested. The Mussar masters describe how fostering growth in *middot* is the pathway that leads to true *binah.*

Your efforts to cultivate the traits that figure on your personal soul curriculum will bring into your life more of the type of understanding of which only the heart is capable.

PRACTICE

An understanding heart comes from the work you do to clear the blockages that result from *middot* that abide in you in excess or deficiency.

You may be aware of a *middah* (a soul-trait) that leads you away from the profound spiritual understanding of which your heart is capable. It's usually not hard to identify one, because that particular trait—whether stinginess or ingratitude or worry or arrogance or whatever it might be—causes stumbling and suffering in your life.

Identify one such soul-trait and give that *middah* extra special attention in this period:

- Study it more.
- Meditate on it longer.
- Chant it with greater passion.
- Journal about it more extensively.

אֵימָה

[5]

Fear

Eima

The terror of a king is like the growling of a lion; He who pro-
vokes him to anger forfeits his own life.

—PROVERBS 20:2

WE DO EVERYTHING to surround ourselves with safety
and security so our lives will be fear free. But our innate
human capacity to experience fear can also play a positive role in
our spiritual lives. There is no virtue in being afraid of mice,
strangers, and your own shadow, yet there are ways to put fear
to use on our path toward wholeness (*shlemut*).

This is not a popular idea—or, as one of my teachers once
said to me, it's a tough sell. Who wants to be afraid? Spiritual
teachers and traditions gain a lot more traction selling peace and
tranquility, because the thought of having more equanimity in
our lives and more inner *shalom* (peace) is so appealing. Yet we
come into this world equipped with a capacity for fear. How can
we put that emotion to good use on the spiritual path?

The starting point is acceptance of the fact that no matter
how high the level of refinement and purification you achieve in

37

your spiritual life, you will never be free of fear. We learn that lesson from a story in the Talmud that describes Moses receiving the Torah from God, in mortal fear.

The Bible describes Moses ascending Mount Sinai to receive the tablets of the law. The story culminates with these words: "Moses went inside the cloud and ascended the mountain; and Moses remained on the mountain forty days and forty nights."[1] Then the scene shifts back to the Israelite camp.

The rabbis of the Talmud were not content to have Moses disappear into the cloud. They wanted to know what happened next, what took place when Moses actually received the Torah. And so we have a teaching of Rabbi Yehoshua ben Levi, who fills in the picture:[2]

When Moses ascended on high, the ministering angels spoke before the Holy One, blessed be He: "Sovereign of the Universe! What business has a mortal among us?" The Holy One answered: "He has come to receive the Torah." The angels replied: "That secret treasure, which has been hidden by You for nine hundred and seventy-four generations before the world was created! You desire to give that to flesh and blood! What is man, that You are mindful of him, And the son of man, that You visit him? O Lord our God, How excellent is Your name in all the earth!" [Psalms 8:5,6,10] Who has set Your glory [i.e., the Torah] upon the Heavens!"

The Holy One said to Moses: "Answer them."

Moses replied: "Sovereign of the Universe. I fear lest they consume me with the [fiery] breath of their mouths."

The Holy One said: "Hold on to My Throne of Glory, and answer them."

Moses then spoke before the Holy One and the angels.

The narrative in the Talmud continues, and Moses picks up more and more confidence to confront the angels, but we already have what we need here. Moses was the greatest prophet of the Jewish people, who, according to tradition, had cleared forty-nine of fifty gates of purification that a human being can pass through. And receiving the Torah was the highest spiritual moment in Jewish history. What do we learn about Moses's experience at that moment? The story tells us he felt afraid.

Moses was so spiritually elevated that he could converse with angels, and if he still experienced fear, this pretty much ensures that you and I down here on earth can expect fear to be a note that will continue to sound in our lives for all time. That just seems to be realistic. We're stuck with fear, so what positive use can we make of it?

Jewish sources tell us that fear can act as a fence to keep us from doing things we really shouldn't. In his famous *Mussar Letter,* Rabbi Yisrael Salanter writes, "The calamities of this world are sorrowful; however, the punishments of sin are far more severe." We should fear those punishments because "the healing remedy for all the ills of the soul is the focusing of man's heart and soul on the fear of punishments taught in the Torah."[3]

Fear of consequences can be a motivator to help us straighten up our ways. When we are confronted by the temptation to do things that we know we really should not do, if all we have to rely on to stop us is good thoughts, we're doomed. No matter how correct or wise, thought is just too flimsy to withstand the emotional power of desire. But if we cultivate a healthy fear of the results of doing wrong, that can be a tool we employ to help us resist the temptation. Equipping ourselves to meet one emotional force (desire) with another (fear) offers us a chance of success.

This is not an easy teaching to embrace. Fear of retribution has much less power in this generation than it did in the past. Perhaps that's because we have moved away from using threats and fear to motivate obedience in the home and in school, too. Or perhaps it's because our lives are generally insulated from the traditional scourges of war, pestilence, and famine, and as technology and medicine conquer one threshold after another, this world starts to look pretty good. As a result, we don't give much thought to what lies ahead, beyond this life, and fear of punishment for transgressions seems not much of a force to help us move our lives in the right direction.

But Rabbi Yisrael writes more: "This is the sum total of all a person's work in service to the Blessed One—to contemplate the fear of heaven contained within the fear of punishment."[4] Here he has introduced another level of fear for us to work with. Fear of punishment contains within it a greater fear, the fear of heaven itself. To be one who fears heaven[5] is the deeper goal.

"Fear of heaven" is a catchphrase that conveys a concept of a person's place in the world. We are human, mortal, limited, and vulnerable in a universe dominated by vast and potent material and spiritual forces and powers. One who fears heaven affirms and accepts that he or she has personal free will and responsibility, that there is a Divine Will at work in the world, and that there is justice in this universe. To be one who does not fear heaven is to deny those fundamental principles of Judaism.

That fear of heaven is the marker of these deeper fundamental Jewish principles helps us understand why the final verse of the book of Ecclesiastes, 12:13, sums up with, "This is the end of the matter, all having been heard: Fear HaShem and keep God's commandments, for this is the whole of a person." Failure to fear heaven exaggerates the scope of our human might and majesty, and so this form of fear is the litmus test of one's faith.

Rabbi Moshe Chaim Luzzatto (1707–46) in the Mussar classic *Path of the Just* gives us another take on the spiritual value of fear. One who fears heaven ought not be concerned so much with punishment from God's big stick but with offending against the supernal glory that infuses our world. This is not fear of breaking a rule and catching the consequences, but rather acting in an unseemly way that besmirches the most precious, pure, and holy divine majesty, which, if we are sensitive to it, permeates every fragment of the reality within which we live.

Rabbi Luzzatto advises us to fear what effect our actions may have on the purity of the divine glory that surrounds us. He says that a person should constantly be "fearing and worrying that some trace of sin might have intruded itself into his actions or that they contain something, small or great, which is inconsonant with the grandeur of the Blessed One's honor and with the majesty of His Name."[6] How could you not fear the misstep that would cause your life to get out of alignment with the Holy?[7]

Every day in the prayers in the daily liturgy we affirm that the whole world is filled with God's glory. God's glory is hidden in our world, but not very obscurely. If you look with the right eyes, it is there to be seen in nature and all life, in the sky and the water, in the hills and the city streets, in the look of an eye, the touch of a hand. Would you want to besmirch such majesty? Wouldn't it be warranted to be afraid of doing just that? Wouldn't the world be a better place if that sort of fear motivated more people to do good in place of evil?

About a thousand years ago, when the Mussar classic *Duties of the Heart* was composed in Spain by Rabbi Bahya ibn Paquda, he reflected on the verse from Proverbs with which this chapter begins. He points out how fearful a person would be of incurring the wrath of a mortal king. How much more should we experience fear that our words or deeds will cross the line of goodness in regard to the King of kings?

PRACTICE

A well-known teaching of the Talmud tells us, "Everything is in the hands of Heaven except the fear of Heaven."[8] It is up to you to decide whether and how you are going to fear heaven. As we learned from Rabbi Luzzatto, what we should fear is not the punishment that will follow a sin but rather sinning itself, which is like tracking mud across God's clean and gleaming kitchen floor.

How do we make fear of sin practical? Rav Kook says that when we contemplate the Infinite in order to feel awe and reverence, the experience leaves a sublime mark on the soul. "When the mind's inner image of reverence expresses itself externally in the world of deeds, it produces a practical revulsion from sin."[9]

Our practice for this period is to get in touch with an inner image of the Infinite by contemplating how many stars there are in the sky. Do you know? Current estimates set the number of stars at nine billion trillion. That number is impossible to conceive. We have to take it in steps.

Slowly set your mind to grasp a grouping of one hundred stars. Then a thousand. Ten thousand. One hundred thousand. One million.

A billion stars equals one thousand million, or 1,000,000,000.

A trillion is a thousand billion, or 1,000,000,000,000.

These are not just numbers. Each one is a brilliant world. But you are still not there, because the number we are seeking involves multiplying a billion by a trillion—nine times!

Sit with your eyes closed to experience the inner image of that inconceivable vastness.

Then ask yourself, in a universe of such enormous complexity, order, and wonder, how can I be so arrogant and self-centered as to sin? In contrast, Rav Kook concludes, if we avoid transgressions, "we can ascend the path towards the sublime light from the Source of life."[10]

יראה

[6]

Awe

Yirah

And now, O Israel, what does the Lord your God ask of you but
to have *yirah* of the Lord your God . . . .

—DEUTERONOMY 10:12

S OME THINGS we learn through the mind and others through
the heart. *Yirah* is an experience of the heart that has the
power to transform.

When translated into English, the word *yirah* can mean
variously "fear" or "awe" or "reverence." It can also describe a
single emotional experience that is woven from all three of these
inner states, for which there is no word in English. On the door-
step to the Promised Land, when Moses delivers his final lessons
to the Jewish people before he dies, he provides them with a list
of five processes or "duties of the heart" that will connect a person to God, the first of which is to have *yirah*. Moses's message
changes significantly depending on which translation we apply.

The spiritual value of fear was explored in our last chapter.
When we switch to thinking of *yirah* as reverence, however, we
encounter a very different message about how to motivate spiri-

44

tual living. The prophet Isaiah (6:3) teaches that the whole world is filled with divine glory. Once your eyes are open to perceiving the presence of the divine everywhere and in everything, what moves you to pursue holiness in your life is not fear of the retribution that will befall you as a result of wrong actions but rather the recognition that you are living in a holy world that is a blessing and a gift. You'd want to do everything you can to prevent being the cause of any defilement within this holy and precious world. This is a case of hewing to the good because we want to live in a way that is consistent with the beauty and perfection that we see all around us.

The reverence we are talking about is summed up by the Talmud in a phrase: "Know before whom you stand."[1] That phrase is often prominently displayed in synagogues, but the point is to make it a feature of your way of life. When you stand in line in the supermarket, or at the seniors' home with your elderly parents, or the day care, or as you wait for your car to be serviced, know that that place, too, is infused with holiness and the glory of God. Internalize that teaching and your every moment is turned into an opportunity to elevate your consciousness.

Yirah can also mean awe. We all have moments of overwhelming, incomprehensible experience in which we transcend the self. Time stands still, and the ordinary boundaries that contain life dissolve in a jaw-dropping revelation of the vast and timeless present, scintillating and luminous.

That luminosity refers to the special quality of divine light that is mentioned again and again in many spiritual traditions. The kabbalists speak of the *Or Ein Sof*—the Light of the Infinite. Rabbi Avraham Yitzchok Kook was perhaps the most vocal in expressing as a vision of reality a world basking in divine light, if only we would have eyes to see. "Human being! See the light of the Divine Presence that pervades all existence. Observe the harmony of the heavenly realm. See how it pervades every aspect of the material and spiritual life which is before our eyes of flesh and our eyes of spirit."[2]

But awe is more than a delightfully illuminated sensation; it is also an experience of the numinous, the word academics use to name the holy. Awe is a vertiginous experience that wells up within when we are in closer connection to the nameless, timeless, and formless that we call the holy, or sometimes God or *HaShem,* which literally means "the Name," the ironic title given to that which we cannot name.

The Mussar teachers tend to refer to God with the name *Ribbono shel Olam*—Master of the Universe. In the Presence of the very source of our existence, we are not to flee or hide, but bend our knee in worship and lend our hearts to serve and our lips to sing praises, just as the verses say we should.

And there is yet more, because there are situations in which it is possible to feel fear and reverence and awe in one single, combined inner experience. Imagine, for example, standing at the very lip of a grand valley, looking down into the vast, deep, and magnificent landscape. Wouldn't you feel dread at the sheer drop into the yawning abyss, dumbfounding astonishment at the beauty of the vast and colorful scene, and maybe also awareness of the divine majesty that permeates this magnificent world?

Or as you gaze out at the trillions of stars reaching billions of light years into the night sky, are you not awed by the immensity of space and simultaneously terrified by the realization of just how small and fragile you really are in such a vast expanse? In the face of the incomprehensible distances of time and space, have you also felt reverence for the mysterious source of this unfathomable universe, just as the opening line of Psalm 19 says,

"The heavens declare the glory of God; the skies proclaim the work of His hands"?

In the story of Jonah, when Jonah was sleeping in the hold of the boat and a great storm blew up, the verse tells us about the sailors, "Then the men had *yirah* for the Lord exceedingly."[3] Have you ever been engulfed in a great storm when your inner experience is simultaneously charged with awe at the tumultuous forces of nature and fear for your own safety, mixed in with an acute awareness of the profound majesty of nature and creation?

These examples point to an experience in which the three emotions that are sometimes called *yirah* are all present simultaneously, with no boundary separating them. Rather, in those special moments, these emotions weave together to create one unified inner state of awe-fear-reverence. You are likely to have had just such an experience, as in the examples I have given or in some other situation. This feeling of being overwhelmed by a reality so much greater than yourself draws back a curtain that ordinarily masks the profundity of life, and you, the little human being, are pierced by a trembling awareness that life is astounding in its reality, vastness, complexity, order, power, and mystery. The natural emotional response to this insight combines terror and awe and reverence all at once—what Jewish tradition calls *yirah*.

Yirah experiences are inherently transformative, which may be why the Psalm tells us that *yirah* is the foundation of wisdom.[4] When the Jews received the Torah at Mount Sinai, there was thunder and lightning and the mountain shook and smoked. Rav Yerucham Levovitz explains that this show of awe-inducing phenomena was not just a dramatic backdrop but a necessary condition for hearing the words of the Torah.[5] The intellect hears and perhaps understands the words, but it is the experiences of the heart that forge in us a new way of being.

PRACTICE

Certain situations or experiences call forth awe without any effort at all. Witness a whale breaching or an eagle soaring, hear a baby's first cry or look upon a magnificent sunset, and the heart responds and connects.

Those "free samples" of awe take no effort, but if we want to train the heart to open to awe, then we must undertake some practice. It needs to be clear, though, that cultivating the capacity to experience awe requires not that you seek out the spectacular, but rather that you endeavor to find the spectacular in everything.

Right now, fix your eye on something that is in your immediate environment. It could be a flower or a pencil, a table or a teacup. Just look at that object until you can sink your consciousness into its very essence, so that you experience how truly remarkable it is that it exists at all. See its material and color and its orderly composition that converge in the altogether miraculous fact that this discrete thing exists in the world. How remarkable! How inconceivable! How awesome!

Repeat this exercise as many times in this period as you are able.

עֲנָוָה

[7]

Humility

Anavah

Before his downfall the heart is proud, but humility comes before honor.

—PROVERBS 18:12

IN COMMON ENGLISH, to call someone humble is to say they
are meek, quiet, unobtrusive, and basically a negligible presence. The Hebrew term for humility conveys none of that.[1]
Rather, it means knowing who you really are and accepting
that truth, if only as the starting point for change. Rabbi Leib
Chasman (1867–1931), Mussar supervisor at the Chevron Yeshiva in Jerusalem, explained that it is not humility to deny who
you are—that is actually just foolishness! Being humble means
knowing the precise truth of your own capacities and accomplishments without any hint of inflation or deflation.

I've previously defined *humility* as "occupying your rightful
space." The ideal is to be so clear on who you are and your place
in your own life that you neither inflate beyond what is real
(we'd call that arrogance) nor retract from filling out the space
that is yours to occupy (self-nullification). Space, in this

context, can be physical but also emotional, psychological, financial, and so on. It is as much a spiritual obstacle to occupy more space around you than is warranted as it is to hold back on making your presence felt to the full extent of your potential.

Humility therefore involves having a true and accurate vision of yourself. Many factors and forces pull us away from that truthful accuracy, and none so much as our own ego. Ego is the lens through which we perceive all of life; and if there happens to be any distortion in that lens—whether giving too grand or too insignificant a vision of who we are—then our outlook on everything will be corrupted. That's what makes humility so fundamental to spiritual life.

The story of Moses well illustrates the role of ego in spiritual life. The Torah describes Moses as "more humble than any other person on the face of the earth."[2] What we know of Moses's life and character before he encountered God at the burning bush and received the order to lead the Israelite slaves to freedom from Egypt tells us that he was not a meek, unassertive, cowering figure. What made him humble then?

Although raised in the pharaoh's palace, when Moses sees a Jew being flogged, he strikes and kills the Egyptian taskmaster.[3] Soon after, he intervenes to prevent a slave from beating a fellow Jew.[4] He runs away to Midian, and there he saves a group of shepherdesses from being harassed by the shepherds.[5] What connects all these stories is that Moses did not make a priority of his own interests; we find his humility in the fact that he was not self-serving.

Another important Jewish leader praised for his humility was Rabbi Yehuda ha'Nasi, who accomplished the monumental task of compiling the text of the Mishnah.[6] It is recorded in the Talmud that when Rabbi Yehuda died, "humility [anavah] . . . ceased to exist."[7] The implication is that this teacher had so perfected his humility that no one else would ever display humility that could match his.

Immediately following this announcement of the demise of humility, Rav Yosef disputes the claim, saying, "Don't say *anavah*," by which he means that humility did not disappear with the sage's death. What reason does Rav Yosef give? "There is still me," he says. Rabbi Yehuda haNasi may have died, but I, Rav Yosef, am still here to show the world what great humility looks like.

What could Rav Yosef possibly have been getting at here? Would a humble person proclaim his own humility? Rav Yosef seems to be demonstrating a lack of the very humility he claims. He is like the man who was given an award for his humility. No sooner had he accepted it than it was taken back!

Some say that Rav Yosef was making a self-deprecating joke. Rabbi Naftali Tzvi Yehuda Berlin (1817–92),[8] however, accepts Rav Yosef's statement at face value. As we've already discussed, an *anav* (humble person) is not someone who sees himself or herself as a nobody but rather is fully and accurately aware of his or her status or level. Perhaps Rav Yosef's statement was true. Maybe he actually was humble, and he knew it.

A true *anav* acknowledges his or her gifts and accomplishments yet takes no credit for them. A fact is just a fact; why should it be a source of pride? Even when we know that we have done something great, we ought to ask, what was the source of this greatness? Did I do it all myself? If what I did took great mental prowess, did I create my brain with its neurons and synapses? If the task took physical strength, did I make my body and its bones and muscles? If the excellence was in the area of courage, did I make my own heart? And so on. In reality, how much credit for success can a person validly take? You don't have to probe very deeply to discover that there is never a tangible basis for seeking honor and certainly not for seeing oneself as somehow better than other people.

The same approach applies to failure. In many cases, a venture does not succeed because of circumstances. Or, indeed, a person may simply have come up short of his or her ambitions. For every Olympic gold medalist there are hundreds and maybe thousands of hard-working and competent "failures." Should a person curse for being two inches shorter than the competitor? Or because his or her parents escaped to a new land where they sacrificed to provide for the family and were unable to afford the Ivy League education that undergirded someone else's success? How much responsibility for failure should someone validly take?

The exception to this rule is moral failure. Our ethical life is the only area where we ourselves are fully responsible, no matter the circumstances or causal factors. But aside from that, where we succeed and where we fail does not need to be received with ego-based reactivity. It is just the cumulative result of so many factors playing through us, many of them beyond our influence.

Our humble Rav Yosef provides insight into this aspect of humility, as well. The Talmud tells us, "Rav Yosef applied to himself [the verse]: 'Much increase [of grain] is by the strength of the ox.'"[9] You can imagine the farmer looking out over mounds of harvested grain. Should he feel personal pride in that harvest when his success is the result of the labor of an ox (or whatever other factors went into creating the successful situation)? Rav Yosef was aware of his virtues, but he saw them as endowments he did not create or own but rather received with gratitude and humility.

Rabbi Moshe Chaim Luzzatto, whose book *Path of the Just* is a pillar of Mussar thought, reveals one more facet of humility.[10]

Not only can one not take credit for the blessings that show up in one's life, but those blessings are actually not gifts so much as obligations:

> One who is wealthy may rejoice in his lot, but at the same time he must help those in need. If one is strong, he must assist the weak and rescue the oppressed. The situation is analogous to that of a household where there are different servants assigned to different tasks, and where each servant must fulfill his appointed task if the affairs and requirements of the household are all to be attended to. In truth, there is no place for pride here.

His conclusion: There is no justification for pride even where there is wealth, strength, or other blessings. The same holds for the inverse situation: There is no basis for shame in poverty, weakness, or a life of challenges.

The Talmudic sage Rabbi Yehoshua ben Levi finds, "Humility is greater than all other virtues, for it is said in Scripture, 'The spirit of God is upon me; because God has anointed me; God has sent me as a herald of joy to the humble.'"[11] We learn here that the "herald of joy" is not sent to anyone other than the humble. The ego is hungry and insatiable, and, as long as we let the ego be our guide and our goal, we will not know joy. We can also see that Isaiah understood why he had no reason to take pride in his accomplishments—no talents, gifts, or abilities are self-created; they come from God.

The great Mussar teacher of the nineteenth century, Rabbi Simcha Zissel Ziv, often quoted Socrates: "I know that I know nothing." He concluded, "The essence of being wise is to know that you aren't. You should be among the humble ones 'who learn from everyone' [*Pirkei Avot* 4:1]."[12]

PRACTICE

Humility has nothing to do with backing away from your talents and accomplishments. As you go through the days of this period, be on the lookout for things you do well. These don't need to be spectacular accomplishments. Perhaps you have a good eye for matching colors, and so your clothing always coordinates. Or maybe your tall stature makes it easy to reach things on upper shelves. Do you easily complete the crossword puzzle? Or tend to find good routes for your drive through town? You have a way with cooking? You tell a good joke?

Having identified what you do well, break down for yourself what talents and abilities go into that accomplishment. Ask yourself questions like those listed here:

- Did I create the eye that matches colors so well?
- Was it me who made my body tall enough to reach up to high places?
- What role did I play in installing synapses in my brain that connect clues to words?
- Isn't my sense of direction a gift I didn't earn?
- Did I implant taste buds in my tongue?
- What did I do to develop a sense of humor?

These are examples. In doing this practice, pay attention to things you accomplish and then ask yourself, in what way am I responsible for these qualities that reside in me? Are they not gifts I have received?

שמחה

[8]

Joy

Simcha

To the straight of heart—joy!

—PSALMS 97:11

THE WORLD is enthralled with happiness, but joy is a much more worthy goal. What's the difference? Getting what you want gives happiness. Once you've enjoyed that gratification, however, the pleasure inevitably dissipates. Joy, on the other hand, dances in the territory beyond want. Happiness is contingent, while joy is unconditional.

To put the distinction another way, happiness involves a person's body, ego, or mind, because those are the dimensions of our selves in which we generally have wants and seek satisfactions. Joy, in contrast, fills the heart only when one gets beyond the wants of the body, ego, or mind to connect more deeply and more intensely with beingness beyond oneself.

We carry on as if we were truly separate entities, but that is a very lonely and, to a degree, illusory way to live. When two people love each other, they no longer exist as separate beings because what we call love is actually a knitting together of souls. We learn that lesson directly from the story of David and Jonathan, about whom the Torah says, "The *nefesh*-soul of Jonathan was knit to the *nefesh*-soul of David, and Jonathan loved him as himself."[1]

Connecting to another person with such thoroughgoing intimacy gives rise to joy, as in the ideal marriage. But the "other" need not be a person. Psalm 140:13 teaches that "the upright will live in Your presence," referring, of course, to God. Being aware at any moment of being in the presence of the Divine opens up the pathway of the heart to ultimate joy.

We can see that joy is much more profound and lasting than happiness. Joy is not so fleeting, because it arises out of profound connection, not a moment of gratification.

An inevitable corollary is that it is impossible to know joy without also being party to the sorrow of the other. Joy rests on such an intimate connection that when the other is hurt, it is your own hurt, as well.

Joy is precious, and we are fortunate that no secret is made of how to find it. Psalms 97:11 puts it simply: "To the straight of heart—joy!" Psalms 32:11 advises, "Be glad in HaShem, and rejoice, you righteous; and shout for joy, all you straight of heart." The connection between having a straight heart and experiencing joy is made clear for us. Seeking joy, all you need to do is straighten your heart. Ah, but just what does that mean and entail?

At a minimum, straightening the heart refers to being morally and emotionally upright. Proverbs 2:15 tells us of "the ways of wicked men . . . whose paths are crooked and who are devious in their ways." The righteous possess a straight inner life, while an inner world that's kinked and bent will never give rise to joy. Our model is the patriarchs and matriarchs of the Torah, who are referred to as "straight."[2] In fact, the traditional name for the Book of Genesis is *Sefer Yesharim*—the Book of the Straight Ones.

Here we are squarely in the territory of Mussar. Those inner convolutions that will keep someone from experiencing joy are none other than that person's personal spiritual curriculum. A tendency to be impatient is an inner kink. So, too, is miserliness. Another type of snarl arises from worry, just as laziness knots up that inner pathway. The baseline for straightening the heart is doing the personal study and practice that have been the focus of the Mussar teachers and their teaching for centuries. "I rejoice in following your statutes as one rejoices in great riches."[3]

But there is more to straightness of heart than just being morally and emotionally unimpeachable, admirable and desirable as that is. Rav Kook teaches that the phrase "straight of heart"[4] refers to people whose hearts and desires are at one—that is, in a straight line—with the Divine Will. Aligning your own heart with God's Will makes it possible to experience joy in this world. Rav Kook is saying that a person who pursues his or her personal wants can hope at most to achieve momentary happiness. But if you "make God's Will your will,"[5] then the deeper, fuller, more resonant experience of joy will permeate your heart.

Maybe you'd really like to be rich or famous. Maybe you'd like a fancy car or watch. Maybe you dream of vacationing like a movie star. And let's imagine you actually achieve your goal. What then? You'll enjoy a brief period of happiness followed by a pretty sharp slope downward until the money or fame is a burden, the car is dented, the watch just reminds you of how little you are doing that day, and the vacation is a distant memory. Then the cycle of craving begins again. That point is actually embedded in the English word *happy,* which shares the same root as the words *haphazard, hapless,* and *happenstance*—all implying momentary chance.

Contrast that way of living to orienting your life to the Divine Will. Sometimes that can mean accepting situations or limitations, but if you think that implies passivity, just consider the real goal God sets for us, which is clearly and succinctly articulated in the Torah as "You shall be holy."[6] As much as we can know anything about God's Will, that's as clear a directive as we are likely to receive. Rav Kook teaches that if you make the pursuit of holiness your own goal, you will have aligned your heart with the Divine Will. Joy then arises spontaneously, or, as a wise person once noted, "When the flowers bloom, the bees come by themselves."

And what is this joy that is the reward of living with a straight heart? I can't improve on the description I gave it in *Every Day, Holy Day:*

> Moments come when the heart dances in the light. So much more than the experience of fun or even happiness, joy erupts when the inner sphere scintillates in its completeness. An experience touches us to the depths of our souls, and in that moment we are graced with a vision—if only fleetingly—of the flawless wholeness and perfection of it all. Then the heart fills and flows over, even amid the brokenness of this world.

The promise of joy is profound. Psalms 107:42 says, "The upright will see and glow." In Hebrew, as in some other Semitic languages, there is a connection between words that mean light and those that mean sprouting, as, for example, *glow* and *grow* in English.[7] It's not a play on words but the actual meaning of the Hebrew to derive from this that the straight of heart will grow. Because we already know that straightness of heart generates joy, joy is identified as the catalyst for spiritual growth. Does this not answer the question posed in Ecclesiastes 2:2, "And of joy, what does it do?"

PRACTICE

Joy is our spiritual fuel and also the catalyst that internalizes our growth, but how do we bring ourselves to experience joy? Isn't it just a spontaneous experience that lands on us unexpectedly, like a colorful bird fluttering down to alight on a branch? Actually, we can cultivate joy by identifying where our heart is crooked and working to straighten the bend.

Are you perpetuating a deceit? Are you acting in a hypocritical way? Are you hiding something? Are you avoiding a truth?

Be honest with yourself and identify one real kink in your inner life. Reference the newspapers for a full range of examples.

Now, what would it take to be relieved of that twisted way of being? What keeps you from letting it go? Give this careful consideration, and see if you can find a way to straighten the knot. I guarantee that you will feel joy if you do.

שימוש חכמים

[9]

Serving the Sages

Shimush Chachamim

Serving the sages is greater than studying from them.

—*BERACHOT* 7B

O UR GOAL is not just intellectual learning but personal transformation, and, in line with that, we are guided here not only to learn from the wise people we encounter in our lives but also to serve them. We are advised that it isn't enough to take their lessons while standing at a distance; we must get up close and interact with our teachers in helpful ways. By doing that, we will not only learn what they have to teach us, we will also observe them close up with our own eyes. A truly wise person has assimilated wisdom into the very fiber of his or her being, and it shows up in every detail of how he or she lives. When we serve our teachers, we experience for ourselves how transformed a person can be.

When King Yehoshafat was seeking a prophet, he was told about Elisha, "who poured water on the hands of the prophet Elijah."[1] The Talmud derives from this verse that serving the sages is greater than learning from them.[2] It is surely valuable to study the lessons of the wise people who have come before us, but we take home much more learning from serving a teacher and thereby witnessing the teachings close up—in action and practice.

A student once asked the Mussar teacher Rabbi Yechezkiel Levenstein why listening to recorded lectures seemed to have less impact on him than hearing the same lectures in person. Rabbi Levenstein said that what doesn't come across in a recording is the *tzelem Elohim*—the divine image—that a person possesses.

When you serve your teacher, the lessons you receive include how he or she eats, bathes, helps out with household chores, opens a book, and (as the old story goes) ties his shoes. Being in close contact with someone who is farther along on the path can impress upon you how the person's spirit permeates the details of material life to a depth and with an impact that no book or story ever can.

This method is explained by the metaphor of a match, which needs to be held close to the wick to transfer the flame. The acquisition of Torah requires close contact with those from whom you can learn, and serving your teacher provides that closeness.

But the need for closeness doesn't explain why this method emphasizes that you must *serve* your teachers. The answer is that if you want to learn and grow by following someone else's example, you must first reduce your own ego, as happens when one serves others. We see this quality in Joshua, who, the *midrash* tells us, was chosen to succeed Moses as leader of the children of Israel because he organized the benches and laid out the mats in the study hall.[3]

So important is the act of serving that the Talmud states, "Even if one has studied and is well versed [in Torah and law] but he didn't serve a sage, he will be an ignoramus."[4]

Service as spiritual practice was much favored in the Mussar yeshiva founded by Rabbi Simcha Zissel Ziv.[5] The yeshiva never employed custodial staff; instead, responsibility for cleaning the facility was left in the hands of certain appointed students. Those carefully chosen students were in charge of everything from washing the floors and chopping firewood to drawing water from the nearby river in the winter when the wells froze over. The best students competed for the honor of doing these tasks, and these "privileges" were often auctioned off.

A wealthy German student once enrolled in the yeshiva. After advancing in his studies and his personal growth, he was afforded the "opportunity" to sweep the study hall. By chance, his mother was visiting the yeshiva and found her son sweeping the floor. Enraged, she went to complain to the Alter, saying, "Have you turned my son into a house cleaner!?" "Yes," replied the Alter. "One who sweeps here overturns the world," making a pun of the Yiddish words for sweep (*kert*) and overturn (*iberkert*).[6]

What's involved here is something that Rabbi Yisrael Salanter stressed, which is that *all* real spiritual development takes place through engagement in real-life situations. Studying patience in the quiet of your study is nothing compared to reaching for it on the freeway. Being generous is simple until you are confronted by the open hand. It's easy to love your relatives from a distance. Not only does serving your teacher give you a glimpse of someone to emulate, it also creates real-life situations—including challenges—that can lead to growth.

Once when I went to visit Rabbi Perr, my Mussar teacher, he told me he was busy that day and the only way we could get some time together was if I accompanied him on an errand. That task turned out to be a trip to the supermarket. He doesn't usually do the shopping, but Mrs. Perr had just had back surgery, so more of the household duties were falling to him. As we entered the grocery store, he got a shopping cart, and I immediately reached over to take control of it. "No," he said. "I have to push it. It's my mitzvah to help my wife when she needs me." Fine, I said, but what about my obligation of serving my teacher? We must have looked quite funny to the other shoppers with the four hands of two big men guiding the cart through the aisles.

PRACTICE

You may not have many opportunities to encounter a "sage" in your everyday life, but there are substitutes. Right now, in your mind, identify someone who is a teacher to you, to whom you want to be close and from whose example you want to absorb lessons.

Pirkei Avot (4:1) tells us, "Who is wise? One who learns from everyone," and from there we learn that anyone can be your teacher. With that in mind, pick someone you respect and ask yourself, What can I do to serve that person right now? Maybe you are already aware of something you could provide. Or you could pick up the phone to call and ask if there is anything he or she needs. Or just drop by your teacher's home, with the intention to be helpful.

If you think you are too busy to act on this practice, or if every form of service you can think of seems too big or too small, too simple or too complex, beware of the undermining power of rationalizations. There is surely something you can do to be of help and service, if you set yourself to do it. And you are sure to see something and learn something and to grow through the process.

דיבוק חברים

[10]

Closeness to Friends

Dibuk Chaverim

"Give me friendship or give me death."

—CHONI THE CIRCLE-MAKER, *TA'ANIT* 23A

THE WORD *dibuk* comes from the Hebrew root that means "adhere" or "cleave." The modern Hebrew word for "glue" is *devek,* from the same root. *Chaverim* is the common term for "friends" or "companions." Often the focus in spiritual practice is on what goes on within the solitary confines of the personal inner life, but here we have a transformative method that involves connecting to friends and sticking close to them.

In the Talmud we meet Choni Ha'Ma'agal,[1] who was a miracle worker. One day, Choni was walking along the road, when he came across a man planting a carob tree. "How long does it take for a carob tree to produce fruit?" asked Choni. "Seventy years," replied the man. When Choni scoffed at this labor from which the man would surely see no produce, the man retorted, "I found a world that had carob trees growing in it. As my ancestors planted for me, so will I plant for my children."

Choni then fell asleep and slept for seventy years. When he

64

woke up, he saw a man gathering carobs from that very tree. "Are you the man who planted this tree?" Choni asked. "I am his grandson," the man answered. "I must have slept for seventy years!" thought Choni to himself.

He went to his own house, but no one recognized him, and they didn't believe him when he said, "I am Choni the circle-maker." When the same thing happened at the study house, Choni was even more devastated. He could not imagine that he was alive but bereft of the close bonds of friendship of his study partners. He exclaimed, "Give me friendship or give me death!"[2] And with that, he expired.

That's how important friendship is to spiritual life. In *Pirkei Avot* 1:6 we read the advice "Acquire for yourself a friend," and in his commentary to this teaching, the Rambam (Maimonides) refers to Choni as the basis for saying, "A person must acquire someone who loves him, for through this, his deeds and all his affairs will be improved. As the Sages said, 'Give me friendship or give me death.'"

It's too common a story, though, that people seem to commit a kind of suicide by cutting themselves off from other people. They judge others and recoil, or, maybe even more often, they judge themselves and withdraw. Either way, they impose solitary confinement on themselves, even though that is the most severe type of punishment inflicted on prisoners, short of physical harm. We are guided here to recognize that bonding yourself to worthy companions is an essential practice on the spiritual path.

In this regard, Rabbi Shlomo Wolbe taught that there are two parallel worlds, and it is up to us to choose which one we live in.[3] The World of Friendship (*olam ha'yedidut*) brings with it love, joy, tranquility, optimism, harmony, generosity, confidence, and faith. The alternative World of Estrangement (*olam ha'zarut*) is characterized by animosity, anger, blame, resentment, criticism, anxiety, sadness, and fear. The choice of which we live in is ours to make.

Choni chose death rather than live outside the World of Friendship, as defined by his friends in the study hall. If you have ever experienced the study hall in a yeshiva, you will likely have seen hundreds of students studying in pairs, generating a roar of animated discussions, yelling and making impassioned pleas. Decorum is nowhere to be found; in its place, there is sharp dialogue among friends endorsed by much experience and sound logic. The Talmud warns, "Just as fire does not ignite itself, so too, the words of Torah do not endure with a person who studies alone."[4]

Whether in the study hall or in any other area of life, friends can disagree. Perspectives can clash. Words can get heated. In the Talmud, Rabbi Hiyya bar Abba tells us, "Even a father and a son, a teacher and student, who study together become enemies."[5] But that is not the end of the matter. They may fight bitterly in search of truth, but, the Talmud continues, they "do not leave each other until there is love between them."[6] The Alter of Kelm explains that when one resolutely pursues truth, someone who is obstructing the way can appear to be an "enemy." But in the very next instant, as issues are resolved (even if it comes to agreeing to disagree, or accepting that both explanations are plausible), the closest of love emerges.[7]

We gain so much from having friends to accompany us on the spiritual path. The journey is not always smooth or easy. There are bumps, detours, and even dead ends along the way. We stumble and fall. The help and support we receive from our *chaverim* give us strength and remind us of our purpose, and help us to continue to pursue our growth.

This point is made in Ecclesiastes 4:9–10, where we read,

"Two are better than one, because they have a good reward for their toil. For if they fall, one will lift up his fellow. But woe to the one who is alone when he falls and has not another to lift him up."

Having friends is clearly helpful, but we learn from Rabbi Eliyahu Dessler (1892–1953) that the very pursuit of friendship transforms us:

> If I give to someone, I feel close to him; I have a share in his being. It follows that if I were to start bestowing good upon everyone I come into contact with, I would soon feel that they are all my relatives, all my loved ones. I now have a share in them all; my being has extended into all of them.[8]

Here we have not only a comment on the importance of friendship but also a clue as to how to foster closeness with others: give to them. Through generosity, we become connected to our friend, and as we do that with more and more people, our entire world is transformed—and us with it.

One more demonstration of the importance of friends to your spiritual life: In Jewish thought, the inner adversary whose specific role is to challenge and even undermine all good intentions and efforts is known as the *yetzer ha'ra,* the evil inclination. The Talmud advises, "If you happen to meet the *yetzer ha'ra,* you should drag him to the study house. If the *yetzer ha'ra* is stone, then he will melt; if he is iron, he will shatter."[9]

Wouldn't it be better just to abandon that negative inclination by running away? Or standing your ground and fighting it into submission? Not in the Talmud's view, because those stratagems mean dealing with your negative tendencies all by yourself, and that is not likely to be an approach that succeeds.

Rather, take your *yetzer ha'ra* with you to the study house, a place where you will find your friends, to whom you can connect and from whom you can draw strength, as they will draw strength from you in their moment of need.

Rabbi Moshe Leib Sassover (1745–1807)[10] commented that he learned the true nature of friendship from two drunken men sitting together and talking. One asked the other, "Are you my friend?" to which the other responded immediately, "Of course! What do you need?" The first answered back, "Obviously you are not my friend. If you were my friend, you would know what I need!"

If you have a friend like that, who knows you well and is walking beside you toward the holy mountain, then what we learn here is that you ought to stick to that person like glue.

PRACTICE

Choose one friend whom you feel is a good influence on your spiritual life, and make a special effort to connect to that person. The practical aspect of that connection means that you need to send an e-mail, make a phone call, or even seek out that person face to face.

But being in verbal or physical proximity with a person is not the full scope of the connection we are guided to seek. As you reach out to connect with your friend, make that connection as real and soulful as can be.

פלפול התלמידים

[11]

Debating with Students

Pilpul ha'Talmidim

Joshua ben Nun, Moses's chosen attendant, spoke up. "My lord
Moses," he said. "Stop them!" "Are you jealous for my sake?"
replied Moses. "I only wish that all of God's people would have
the gift of prophecy!"

—NUMBERS 11:28–29

J EWS LOVE to argue. Two Jews, three opinions, goes the joke.
There is nothing new in this. The prototype is Abraham
haggling with God over the number of righteous people needed
to save Sodom and Gomorrah from destruction.[1] Moses does his
share of arguing with God, as well. The Talmud is a record of
rabbis arguing, often over other arguments. Talmud study is basically nonstop arguing, and the debate can be so heated that it
is described in military terms, as "the war of Torah."[2]

That the text of the Talmud preserves both the winning and
the minority opinions in the arguments it records tells us that we
are not meant to study it as a source of dogma or even to glean
the bottom-line outcome of arguments. Rather, we who would

learn from them are meant to enter into and engage in the arguments themselves.

This is an astute approach. We learn more and we learn better when we are not given the solution to a question but rather have to work it out for ourselves, in reflection on the text and its commentaries. Forced to argue and struggle with the various sides of an issue, we come to a personal realization of the conclusion that we can then take possession of as our own. Wisdom that takes such deep root has the power to transform us.

The word *pilpul,* which names this method, derives from the Hebrew word *pilpel,* which means "pepper." We're talking about peppery arguments, sharp thoughts, and words that awaken the senses and the mind. The Talmud tells us that when we face the final judgment after death, one of the questions we can expect to be asked and held accountable for is *pilpalta b'chochma?*—Did you explore the pungent details of wisdom?[3]

How sharp is this debating supposed to be? Rabbi Hiyya bar Abba was quoted in the previous chapter as saying that those who argue start out disputing with each other like enemies, "yet they do not stir from there until they come to love one another."[4]

An argument begins with sharp and unrelenting debate but needs to end in a spirit of love. "At that stage," Rabbi Yisrael Salanter writes, "each person nullifies his own opinion in order to follow the majority or the most outstanding sage; or each holds true to his own opinion."[5] Why the initial jousting and confrontation, and why the latterly seeking of resolution in a variety of forms? Because the goal is *truth.* We need to come out swinging on behalf of truth, and we need to surrender (or not!) in light of the truth that emerges from this process.

Of course, not every argument is dedicated to truth. Sometimes people argue simply to win the debate, or to glorify an ego or to claim a prize, hang the truth. Many a criminal has gone free not because they didn't commit the crime but because the defense attorney argued so effectively. In political debate, undermining the other side is likely to be a much higher priority than truth, which may not factor into anyone's calculations.

Jewish tradition distinguishes between arguments that are dedicated to truth and those that aren't. An altruistic argument in pursuit of truth is said to be "for the sake of heaven." That sort of argument delivers lasting results. In contrast, and no matter how beautiful or effective, arguments that are not for the sake of heaven do not turn up any truth that is destined to endure.[6]

Accessing truth, Rabbi Salanter concludes, means discovering that which coincides with the Divine Will. Failure to align with truth leads to thoughts and actions that go against the Divine Will, with dire results. The truth that reflects the Divine Will is meant to emerge not from heaven itself but from the very human process of collaborative debate, conducted with passion and discipline.

There are famous examples where people engage God in argument, and these instances create the template for our own need to argue in order to discern the Divine Will. When God hears how sinful the people of Sodom and Gomorah had been, God reveals to Abraham that both cities and all their inhabitants will be destroyed (*Genesis* 18: 16–33). Abraham then challenges God not to "sweep away the innocent with the guilty" and proceeds to negotiate. Will you spare the city if there are fifty innocent people to be found there, Abraham argues? What if you find forty-five? And so on until God agrees that if ten innocent people can be found in the cities, the decree that they be destroyed will be rescinded.

God also engaged in arguments with Moses. When Moses is on Mount Sinai to receive the Torah and the people down below build a golden calf, God threatens to destroy the nation and start over again with Moses. God said to Moses, "I have seen this people, how stiff-necked they are. Now let me alone, so that my anger may burn hot against them and I may consume them. And of you I will make a great nation" (Exodus 32:9–14). Moses then raises arguments against this plan, pointing out that if God goes ahead and wipes out the nation, the Egyptians will conclude that God brought the people out of Egypt just to kill them in the wilderness. He reminds God of the promises God had made Abraham, Isaac, and Jacob. And God heard the arguments and reversed the plan to destroy the people.

Job is another figure from the Bible who does not take his fate sitting down. From Job we learn the fearlessness that is required to step up and argue: "God may well slay me; I may have no hope. Yet I will argue my case before God" (Job 13:15).

These and other examples tell us that it is not only acceptable to argue with God, but that there are times when those arguments are essential to determining the Divine Will itself. Things unfold the way they do because someone stood up to argue. The Torah describes Abraham as fully righteous but of Noah it says only that he was "righteous in his generation." Abraham is judged more righteous because when God threatened destruction he argued, whereas Noah did not raise his voice and just busied himself building the ark.

If arguing is how we work things out with God, how much more must argument have a vital role in sorting things out within the fallible and uncertain relationships we have with other people?

One question remains. Why is it so important to argue with *students,* more than with peers or spouse or even one's teacher? The same emphasis appears in a statement in the Talmud: "Much have I learned from my teachers, more from my peers, but most

of all from my students."⁷ What special benefit to personal transformation comes from arguing with students?

The Maharal of Prague⁸ (Rabbi Yehudah Loew, 1525–1609)
points out that someone who reaches a high level of wisdom can
be diverted from asking the simple questions that are the basis
for true clarity and continued growth. That never happens when
interacting with a hungry and inquisitive student. He cites the
teaching in the Talmud of Rav Nachman bar Yitzchak, who
asked, "Why are the words of Torah compared to a tree?" And
he answered, "This is to teach you that just as a small piece of
wood ignites a larger one, so it is with scholars: the younger ones
sharpen the minds of the older ones."⁹

We find this point illustrated in the tragic story about Rabbi
Yochanan, who was the teacher of Reish Lakish:¹⁰ So much did
the teacher value the arguments he had with his student that
when Reish Lakish passed away, Rabbi Yochanan was inconsol-
able. The rabbis sent Elazar ben Pedas to comfort him because,
they said, "his scholarship is brilliant." Every time Rabbi Yochanan raised an argument, Elazar ben Pedas brought him a
corroborating proof, until R' Yochanan eventually expressed
exasperation. "With Reish Lakish, whenever I would say something, he would pose twenty-four difficulties and I would give
him twenty-four solutions, and as a result the subject became
clear. Of what use is your constantly supporting what I say?
Don't I already know that I have said well?" And R' Yochanan
tore his clothes and cried for his late student until his sanity wore
away from him.

So much did the late sixteenth-century sage known as the
Maharsha¹¹ value give and take with his students that when we
turn to see his commentary on a certain page of the Talmud,¹²
we find that he had nothing to say on that subject. Why? Because when he studied that page, he had been away at the market

in Lublin; and so his ideas had not been refined through a discussion with his students.

PRACTICE

Your practice for this period is to seek opportunities to try to teach something you have learned to someone else and to do so in a "peppery" way. Peppery does not mean rude or mean or untrue or aggressive. It is sharp and pungent. When you teach that lesson, encourage sharp questions.

Watch what happens. It's quite probable that you will find that you didn't have the material quite so clear in your mind as you thought. You'll also likely discover that you yourself learned something else or refined an idea because of the questions you stirred. Your "student" will not be the only one to benefit from the arguments you spark.

ישוב

[12]

Settledness

Yishuv

A person who has mastered peace of mind has gained everything.

—RABBI SIMCHA ZISSEL ZIV, THE ALTER OF KELM

YISHUV can mean dwelling, sitting, or resting. Some commentators understand this quality to be a frame of mind—inner composure and clarity of thought. Others, maybe of a more concrete bent, see this as the quality of sitting down to study, with emphasis on being diligent.

This is such a classic split within Jewish thought and practice. Does the emphasis fall on required behavior (in this case, sitting down to study) or the mental attitude with which the act is done (here, *yishuv da'at*, peace of mind)?

The debate is irresolvable because both positions have merit. But, in this case, I find it more useful to focus on the inner quality of mental calmness, because, without that, a person won't likely be able to fulfill the other goal of sitting diligently. Peace of mind (*yishuv da'at*; literally, seated consciousness) is what permits the persistent and hard-working effort that study and practice require.

The Talmud offers a beautiful image of a settled mind.[1] "Rabbi Nahman bar Yitzchak observed: 'Study requires as much clarity of mind as a day when the north wind blows.'" It then goes on to note how everyday life can impinge on that clear, inner space: "Abaye remarked: 'If my [foster] mother had told me: "Bring me to do a simple task," I would not have been able to study.' Said Rabbah, 'If a louse bit me I could not study.'"

These examples are not as distant from our experience as they might seem. At times, the mind is as clear and calm as a remote lake early on a windless morning. And then along comes a distraction no bigger than an ant or weightier than a thought, and that settled frame of mind is gone in a flash, leaving us churning in consternation in its inner wake.

The mind in conflict with itself is what the fourteenth-century commentator known as the Ran called *tiruf ha'da'at,* the mind state we experience when there is a conflict between the intellect and the emotions.[2] You set yourself in pursuit of a clearly defined goal with a focused and unified mind, and all is calm, until the mosquito bites and the itch distracts. Or a thought pops up seemingly out of nowhere that tickles a desire in you, and a fantasy grows. Or you are visited by a memory of an offense that was done to you, and the pain of that insult returns in force. Peace of mind is an unstable and fleeting experience, and there are any number of candidates available to disrupt that inner balance.

We experience peace of mind when there is no stress or tension between the intentions we set for ourselves and our physical desires or emotional states. Rav Shlomo Wolbe writes that the goal of all personal spiritual practice is to be at peace with oneself, with one's environment, and with God.[3]

Rabbi Eliyahu Dessler explains how to reach that goal.[4] It is impossible to concentrate when outside interests and desires cloud the mind. A settled mind is achieved primarily by *clearing the mind* of all else but the task at hand. He adds that when a person makes a little effort in this direction, he or she is rewarded with Divine assistance, and that through the process of trying to achieve mental settledness, one comes to acquire *menuchat ha'nefesh* (tranquility, a settled soul).

Rav Dessler makes it sound easy—just clear your mind. When we think about doing that, however, it seems so difficult to accomplish. But we only need to begin the process to discover that it is more accessible than it appeared before we made that initial effort. Wouldn't that be just how we'd expect Divine assistance to come to us?

The things that unsettle your mind are seldom random. Each of us is prone to certain kinds of disruptions and distractions. In workshops and retreats, I sometimes assign people to do a simple, mind-focusing meditation that involves concentrating on a single word or image. After the assigned time has elapsed, I ask all those who are willing to say what distracted them. One person may report having a sexual fantasy. Another might say she was thinking about lunch. A third could tell of warming up old embers of envy, and someone else admits to getting lost in planning their whole week.

When the group discusses these distractions, in short order it becomes clear that what unsettles the mind is none other than one's personal spiritual curriculum. The distractions of the mind are usually rooted in the specific *middot* that are in play for that person at that time; these are the soul-traits in which that person has the potential to grow. That's why different people experience different distractions, and the same person tends to find the same kind of thought or feeling recurring as the culprit for distraction. Distractions of mind are not like trash or dirt to be swept away. Rather, they call out a crucial truth about priorities for spiritual practice that one who would ascend in the direction of holiness can find very valuable and useful.

In my own case, what tends to disturb my peace of mind is planning. No sooner does that settled state of inner calm take hold than thoughts of what I'll be doing later today and tomorrow and for the rest of my life come creeping in. That's my pattern, just as you will have your own pattern, if you can become aware of it.

What does planning tell me about my own spiritual curriculum? It reveals weakness in the trait of *bitachon* (trust). When I assign myself to clear my mind, I open an inner space that welcomes my own particular version of anxiety, which is planning the future. Once I discover and acknowledge that worry is the factor that disturbs my peace of mind, I also learn that cultivating trust is the pathway for me to regain my inner settledness.

The personal spiritual transformation that is called acquiring Torah requires that a person be adept at clearing his or her mind from all other matters, whether pressures of work or family, physical ailments, fantasies, worries about the weather, or anything else that creates inner turbulence. A relaxed and focused, peaceful mind, free of distractions, is essential for spiritual growth. The route to that inner state runs directly through the territory of Mussar, where we are guided in the ways of refining our inner traits that they not be obstacles to our spiritual aspirations.

PRACTICE

Mostly our issue with the trait of settledness of mind is lack of it. Rav Kook offers a practice that will return one to a calm state of mind:[5]

When settling your mind is a challenge, he advises a visit to a place of nature to experience "the tranquility that wells up from the goodness of God that fills all of existence: The songs of the birds as they perch in the trees, the views of the beauty of the Carmel and of the Sharon with their pleasant flowers, and the sweet smell of the lilies and the fruit in God's garden on earth that He gave to all humanity. They return one's mind [*da'at*] to its natural state after being distanced from it by culture and society. And in returning to one's source in nature, the creations of God's hands, all the natural pleasantness of one's soul returns to him, including feelings of sanctity and ascendancy of spirit that connects to the Almighty, as well as good character."

Your practice is to seek moments in which to experience a natural environment. Step out into the garden. Pull over to visit that park you drive through every day. Tune into the sounds, colors, and impressions, and observe for yourself what effect that experience has on your peace of mind.

מקרא ומשנה

[13]

Studying the Written and Oral Torah

Mikra & Mishnah

These words which I command you today shall be upon your heart. You shall teach them thoroughly to your children, and you shall speak of them when you sit in your house and when you walk on the road, when you lie down and when you rise up.

—DEUTERONOMY 6:6–9

T HE FIRST METHOD to internalize Jewish wisdom that we explored in this book was *talmud,* translated as "study." How does this current method—studying the written and oral Torah—differ from what we've already learned about study?

The *Sh'ma* is the primary statement of Jewish belief and monotheism, and in the first blessing recited in the *Sh'ma,* we read the instruction that we should lay the words of the Torah on our hearts, and we should teach them thoroughly (*v'shinantam*) to our children. In the teaching from the Talmud quoted in the epigraph above, Rabbi Yehoshua ben Chananya does a little word play to switch the word *v'shinantam* to read *v'shlishtam*,[1] which causes the meaning of the verse to change to "and you shall divide them in thirds." He then deduces that a person should divide learning into three equal portions: biblical scripture (the written Torah), and Mishnah and Gemara, which together compose the Talmud (the oral Torah). (Then along come the commentators to argue whether that means a third of every day, or one day in three, or even one year in three, devoted to each of these subjects.)

The first reference to study we encountered was general, and here we get specifics: To gain access to the transformation wrought by Torah, we must spend time learning both the written Torah (the Bible) and the oral Torah.

In saying that we must study both the oral and written Torah, our teaching is making a political statement. In the period of the Second Temple (between 530 B.C.E. and 70 C.E.), there was division in the Jewish world between the Pharisees, who gave the written and oral traditions equal importance, and the Sadducees, who accorded authority only to the written word (especially the Books of Moses). After the destruction of the Second Temple, the Pharisees came to dominate, and rabbinic Judaism was born. We ourselves are within that tradition that acknowledges both the oral and the written Torah and asserts that we need to study and follow the teachings of both. Most of us, that is. The sect of the Karaites still exists, mostly in Israel, and is made up of people from Iraq and Egypt who traditionally (and to this day) have accepted only the written Torah as their guide.

The dominant view, however, is that acquiring wisdom requires study of *both* the written and the oral traditions, because one cannot be understood properly without the other.

Many teachings of the written Torah just could not be

understood or acted upon without the oral tradition to fill in the picture. In regard to ritual, for example, we get the verse that is incorporated into the blessings after the *Sh'ma:* "You shall tie them as a sign on your arm and for *totafot* between your eyes."[2] Tie what on your arm? Who? How? When? And just what are *totafot,* anyway? We'd have no idea without the oral tradition to explain the practice of wearing *tefillin.*[3]

The oral and the written sources are also needed to understand what is involved in Jewish law. The verse that calls for "an eye for an eye and a tooth for a tooth," for example, would set off a slew of vengeance seeking and retribution, except that in the hands of the rabbis this is understood to be all about monetary compensation, not retaliation.

Emphasizing text study as spiritual practice is a distinctively Jewish element of this path. The Talmud spells this out:

Rav Yosef said, "Torah study is superior to saving lives." Rav, and some say, Rabbi Shmuel Bar Marta, said, "Torah study is superior to the building of the temple." Rebbi said in the name of Rav Yitzchak bar Shmuel Bar Marta, "Torah study is superior to honoring your mother and your father."[4]

This list of things here being compared to Torah study is not random.

Saving a life is usually the trump card in Jewish thought and practice, as nothing is meant to stand in the way of life-saving activities. Torah study is superior.

The temple is the location of the holy of holies, where God's presence was manifest. Torah study is superior.

And honoring one's mother and father is not only one of the

Ten Commandments, it is also the primary obligation in the interpersonal realm, because our parents gave us life itself. And Torah study is superior even to honoring one's parents.

Why does Torah study rank even higher than the elevated status ascribed to each of these three categories of practice? Because when you study Torah, you save your own life because you connect to the source of truth and goodness that is the essence of living. The temple is no longer standing, and so that route to spiritual elevation is simply not available to us today, whereas Torah study is entirely accessible. And there is no higher way to honor one's parents than to become someone who embodies the highest ideals they would hope for us, which we learn from Torah.

PRACTICE

Let's do some learning to see how the oral tradition is needed to understand and fulfill the verses of the Torah. The prayer book quotes a Mishnah that is set before us to learn every day: "These are the precepts that have no prescribed measure: the corner of a field, the first fruit offering, the pilgrimage, acts of kindness, and Torah study."[5] The Mishnah is elucidating verses from the Torah that we can break out, one by one:

The Corner of a Field

Leviticus 19:9–11 tells us that the corners of fields (*pe'ah*) are designated for the poor: "When you [plural] reap the harvest of your land, you [singular] shall not reap all the way to the corner of your field, or gather the gleanings of your harvest. You shall not pick your vineyard bare, or gather the fallen fruit of your vineyard; you shall leave them for the poor and the stranger."

No specific measurement is provided to determine how much of the field to leave unharvested.

The First Fruit Offering

Deuteronomy 26:2 describes the offering of the first fruits: "You shall take of the first of every fruit of the ground that you bring in from your Land that your God gives you, and you shall put it in a basket and go to the place that your God, will choose . . . ." No limit is set for how much fruit is to be offered.

The Pilgrimage

Rayon refers to being seen to be a pilgrim who goes up to the Temple for the three commanded annual visits, at the festivals of Pesach, Shavuot, and Succot. No specific amount of time is set that a pilgrim must spend in Jerusalem, nor for how many sacrifices must be brought.

Acts of Kindness

It is said that the Torah begins with an act of kindness (God clothing Adam and Eve) and ends with an act of kindness (God burying Moses). There is no limit or end to the kindnesses we can do in our life to those around us and those in need, such as visiting the sick, clothing the naked, and feeding the hungry.

Torah study

Torah study is a commandment, but how many hours or days or years is nowhere stipulated.

Now that you have learned a bit of Mishnah and the scripture upon which it is based, go back and review what you have learned.

[14]

Purity

Tahara

Who can say, "I have kept my heart pure; I am clean and without wrong-doing"?

—PROVERBS 20:9

OF COURSE, being pure is a prerequisite for the transformation that is called acquiring Torah. How could the holy
and the defiled possibly occupy the same space? But what do we
mean by "pure" in a spiritual sense, and what is entailed in being
pure? The Hebrew word for "purity" is *tahara,* but we must be
careful not to leap to the conclusion that we understand *tahara*
just because we can make sense of the English word *purity.* The
two concepts overlap, but they do not coincide.

Purity is stressed in many places in the Bible, and we do find
that some issues of impurity can be dealt with by washing or
immersion in water, as if to remove a stain.[1] But there are other
sorts of defilement that are intrinsic to an entity, and no matter
how hard we scour, we won't ever be able to change them. Only
fish with scales are deemed edible, for example, and as a result,

no amount of scrubbing will turn a catfish pure. Traditional Jewish notions of purity and impurity invoke a metaphysical reality that is very different from the bacterially based concept of cleanliness most of us live with today.

As far as people go, our default position is to be pure, and it's only because of certain circumstances that we are knocked out of that state of affairs. The commentators[2] spend more time focused on *tahara*'s opposite, which is *tumah,* and this makes sense, because, in most cases, what they are concerned with is a kind of spiritual contagion that renders the pure impure by contact. We are pure until something happens to move us out of that status.

The Hebrew word *tumah* is generally understood to derive from a root that means to be "entombed." Corpses (human and otherwise) are, indeed, the most common source of impurity, but that connection to death is confounded when we include giving birth and having contact with bodily fluids (including life-giving ones) among the ways a living person can become impure. What brings about impurity are metaphorical or spiritual conditions that involve the material but are not limited to it. Someone becomes "entombed" in life by doing something or encountering something that causes him or her to become walled off, which in this context means spiritually disconnected.

The lesson here is that when we touch things we shouldn't or do things that are defiling in the material realm, we become tainted; and the soul gets cut off from its spiritual root and sustenance.

We can put this notion to use. A person or object is pure when uncontaminated by anything that would interfere with positive connectivity. We so want and need to connect—to our own souls, to other people, and to the Divine Source—that we ought to pay careful attention to anything that will cause us to become walled off from fostering these spiritual bonds.

Rabbi Moshe Chaim Luzzatto defines *purity* as "perfecting one's heart and one's thoughts."³ He draws an analogy from the meal offering that was made in the holy temple, which was sifted thirteen times to ensure that the flour was perfectly pure. He enjoins us to sift our own inner beings to bring our thoughts, words, and deeds to an equally high level of purity.

Most of us can easily identify the sorts of thoughts and feelings that defile our inner purity. Lusting after what ought not be ours, or wishing evil on others who have done nothing to us except to succeed beyond our level, or seeking to glorify ourselves fall into this familiar category.⁴ But that is not where Rabbi Luzzatto focuses. It wouldn't take all that much sensitivity to catch those sorts of thoughts on the first inner sift or two. He moves us along in the process to watch out for the impurities that infect not only the negative things we do but also the positive. The chief culprit here is ulterior motives.

The Mussar teachings on ulterior motives illustrate the careful attention we need to pay to the subtleties of our inner workings and the effort it takes to purify them. "Nothing requires greater insight and effort than keeping away from impure motives," Rabbi Luzzatto writes.⁵ He then compares the ideal of a good deed done entirely for its own sake with one where desire for praise or reward has crept in. And even where there is no desire to be praised, "still, in rejoicing over the praise that he receives, a person might come to take greater pains than he normally would, as in the case of Rabbi Chanina ben Teradyon's daughter, [*Avodah Zarah* 18a] who overhearing some men remark about her graceful stride, saying, 'How beautifully that girl walks,' immediately sought, because of this praise, to display even more grace." He concludes, "Even if the impure motive plays only an insignificant part, the deed which contains such a motive is no longer completely pure."

This sets the standard for our purity. We should not do harmful things, of course. But even the good things we strive to do are susceptible to impurity if we allow corrupt motivations to sneak in. This is the level of self-awareness the Mussar teachers urge us to reach. Sift thirteen times. Seek to be aware of even tiny imprints of self-gratification, exploitation, willful blindness, and ego that will leave their greasy fingerprints on the polished mirror of the soul you are.

What does purity look and feel like? We can only bring out analogies, like the polished mirror. The Talmud suggests another image: the breath of small children engaged in their study in the schoolroom.[6] The innocent and sweet voices of children reflect the purity we who are years past childhood know and feel still exists in us. We need to foster that quality if we would transform.

The Talmud's image of children's voices makes another point, as well. Those innocent voices are not just sweetly pure, they are the glue that keeps the world in existence. What the sage actually said was that "the world endures only for the sake of the breath of school children."[7] Hearing this, the sage Rav Papa said to his colleague Abaye, "What about mine and yours?" Abaye replied, "Breath in which there is sin is not like breath in which there is no sin."

It is up to us to look within and know the difference. What motives are we acting on? How pure are our ideals and our deeds? What stands in the way of our pure connection to soul, other, and divine? What can we do to become purer?

PRACTICE

The full-blown system of *tahara* and *tumah* given to us in the Torah is no longer practiced, and so we are free to seek out the kernel of the concepts and apply them in our own lives. I invite you to do that by reflecting on what you can do to remove impediments to connectivity in your life.

There are many things that can defile our purity, and still we choose them and participate in them willingly, even though they have negative consequences. Food, sexual thoughts, drink, other substances, television, the Internet, some people, and many other things can have a defiling influence on our lives and our souls. Your practice is to recognize any temptations that come before you that have some potential to be defiling, and to respond to them by withdrawing your hand in a conscious act of self-containment. Then choose wisely, seeking the pure and the holy.

Is there an impurity that interferes with your own sense of being connected to your holy essence, your soul? What can you do about that?

Is there impurity between you and another person that you can clean up? What is stopping you?

Is any cleanup needed to purify your relationship with God? How can you be purer?

15

Limiting Sleep

Miyut Shaynah

How long will you lie there, lazybones;
When will you wake from your sleep?
A bit more sleep, a bit more slumber,
A bit more hugging yourself in bed.

—PROVERBS 6:9–10

SLEEP IS A necessity to refresh body and spirit, and some people's dearest prayer is to get a good night's sleep, at least once in a while. Depriving someone of sleep is a very effective form of torture. All you have to do to get someone to tell you anything you want to know is to keep that person awake for forty-eight hours. But the guidance we receive here is to "limit sleep," and that makes clear that the more common situation involves the opposite tendency, which is to sleep to excess.

There are Jewish notions about how much sleep a person should get every night. The Rambam rules that the average adult needs six to eight hours of sleep and notes, "If a person sleeps in order to allow his mind to rest and to give rest to his body so that he should not become sick and unable to serve God because of illness, in this case his very sleep is service of God."[1] Another source cautions, "One who stays awake at night imperils one's own life."[2]

On the other hand, we have the eighteenth-century Vilna Gaon, whose son reported that in the fifty years he knew his father, he never saw him sleep more than two hours per day.[3] That's an extreme example, but there is a tradition on the festival of Shavuot to stay up all night to learn Torah, and in some yeshivas learning all night happens once every week. There is an age-old practice of righteous seekers rousing themselves from sleep at midnight to study Torah and meditate in heartfelt prayers.[4] It's not hard to find the reason: In the Torah we read the direct instruction "Keep this Book of the Law always on your lips; meditate on it day *and night,* so that you may be careful to do everything written in it. Then you will be prosperous and successful."[5]

The Talmud puts it poetically: "The moonlight was created for the study of Torah,"[6] and Rabbi Eliezer adds ominously, "Any home where the words of Torah are not heard at night will be consumed by fire." Some might say that Torah study demands "toil," and that means pushing beyond the comfort zone by forgoing sleep and other comforts. That austere notion is not one that is widely accepted, however. In the Talmud, Rabbi Yochanan rules that a person who takes an oath not to sleep for three days is to be punished with lashes.[7]

Night has its own special energy that invites a more spiritual experience. The quiet and peaceful stillness of the night welcome deeper contemplation, undisturbed by the hustle and noise that clutter the daylight hours. Spiritual growth requires that we access our inner world, and night can offer special opportunities to achieve that.

But leaving aside special nighttime practices, we still should not sleep too much, and the reason is simple: Life is precious, and there is much to do. The Alter of Novarodok quipped, "The trouble with people is that they want to change overnight and have a good night's sleep that night, too." His point is that we sign on for the goal but are often unwilling to make the sacrifices that lead to accomplishing it.

The Alter of Novarodok is here targeting the tendency to be lazy. Because sleep is so necessary to health, it really can't be the issue itself; laziness is. It's laziness that has us spending extra hours under the blanket, beyond the sleep the body needs. Rabbi Moshe Chaim Luzzatto points out that we often know what should be done and are committed to action, but laziness brings us down.[8] We accept (and even manufacture) a myriad of excuses to rationalize our inaction.

Contrast what Rabbi Chaim Friedlander (1923–86), author of *Sifsei Chaim,* reports about that Mussar exemplar the Alter of Kelm, who was near the end of his life and very infirm when he once awoke from a sleep and, realizing that he was still in bed, called out, "*Atzlus!* [Laziness!]" and made an effort to get out of bed. Because he was not lazy, he did not want to spend more time in bed than necessary.

The ultimate source of our tendency to be indolent is the familiar *yetzer ha'ra,* the inner adversary to all our spiritual aspirations. The *yetzer ha'ra* provides all kinds of rationales to justify that extra thirty or sixty minutes of sleep. This is how the *yetzer ha'ra* directs your life—as long as you are asleep (literally or metaphorically), you can't do what's required of you or that to which you aspire.

There is a story told about the Chafetz Chaim, a remarkably humble and accomplished sage of the twentieth century, that concerns his old age. He was blessed to live ninety-five years (from 1838 to 1933), and when he was already in his nineties, as he awoke in the morning, he'd think, "Maybe today you should sleep a little longer. You are already in your tenth decade, you have done so much. You have already had a major influence on the Jewish world. Why not take a few more minutes' sleep? It's still early." To which the Chafetz Chaim would reply, "It can't be so early if *you* are already up," since he knew that the voice he was hearing was not his own but that of the *yetzer ha'ra.*

Each of us needs to get the right amount of sleep to keep our minds and bodies healthy. Less is torture; more is indulgence. The sleep we get at night in bed, however, is not the only form of sleeping we do. We also need to minimize the amount of time we spend asleep even while we are technically awake.

We need to be vigilant not to live our lives as sleepwalkers. On a deep level, the entire teaching of Mussar is about waking up to life. The Rambam explains the commandment to blow the shofar on Rosh Hashana like this:[9]

> Even though blowing shofar on Rosh Hashana is a Divine decree, it contains an allusion. Oh you sleepers! Awaken from your sleep! You slumbering ones from your slumber! Search your ways and repent, and remember your Creator.

Things happen in life that hit us hard and deliver a wake-up call. How much better not to be asleep in the first place! In *Pirkei Avot* 1:14, Hillel says, "If I am not for myself, who will be for me?" If you don't wake yourself up, who will?

PRACTICE

Sleep is not wasted time. The Rambam's view is that the average adult needs between six and eight hours of sleep a night, and most people would agree. Do you know how much sleep you need, with emphasis on the word *need*?

Starting tonight, your practice for this period is to set out to sleep only the number of hours you know you need, be that six, seven, or eight hours, or fractions thereof.

Be very conscious of the choice of hour you make when you set your alarm for your morning wake-up.

That addresses a practice to bodily sleep. Hopefully, that will be a step toward becoming truly awake in your life.

מיעוט שיחה

[16]

Limiting Conversation

Miyut Sichah

In a multitude of words there is no lack of sin, but he that refrains his lips is wise.

—PROVERBS 10:19

SPEECH is a great (and, some would say, defining) human gift. But it has to be used with care. God created the world with the spoken word, yet that same power has done as much harm as (if not more than) swords and bombs.

Miyut sichah literally means "limiting conversation." That does not mean maintaining a vow of silence, because we are supposed to engage in valid spiritual talking, as the Torah itself instructs: "You must speak words of Torah."[1] And it can't be asking us to reduce our gossip and slander, because those negative uses of speech are roundly condemned in Jewish law; so it's not likely that we would be told to "limit" that sort of talking, as if a little is okay, as long as it is not too much.

What the text is asking us to do is cut down on the sort of elective conversation that is actually permitted to us. We are being asked to reduce the small talk as much as possible. It is in

95

our spiritual best interest not to give our attention, our energy, and our tongues to empty nattering.

Most of us actually enjoy making frivolous conversation. We prattle about the weather or the news of the day, the sports scores, or the latest fad. In fact, some people find value in that sort of chitchat, because it allows strangers to make contact and be friendly. It makes people feel they belong to the society in which they are situated. It sometimes even disseminates important information or gives rise to good ideas.

Rabbi Yisrael Salanter was once standing in the marketplace engaging a man in small talk. Rabbi Yisrael made jokes and exchanged witty comments with the other man, who was laughing at his jokes and enjoying himself. Bystanders were astonished. How could Rabbi Yisrael, who was constantly studying Torah and whose heart was always turned to important issues, be spending time kibbitzing in the marketplace?

One of them asked Rabbi Yisrael about this behavior. Rabbi Yisrael explained that he knew that the life of the man he was talking with was filled with sadness, and his soul was overtaken by a dark depression. The only way to lift his burden was with light, pleasant conversation about worldly matters. To provide that was a great act of kindness to the man.[2]

So we see that in this and a myriad of other ways, conversation has an important role to play as a thread that weaves together our human lives. While that remains true, it is also true that excessive trivial babbling can be a complete waste of time and brain power. It may even be an abuse of the precious gift of speech, something akin to using a Rolls-Royce to deliver pizzas.

For one thing, many gifts await us that we can access only in a space of silence, only if we sometimes stop the chatter and interrupt the noise. Rabbi Akiva says, "Silence is a protection for wisdom."[3] Constant banter is not the greatest sign of wisdom. You know that with certainty about other people. Can you see any way in which that notion can be applied to you, as well?

The Maharal explains that speech is a physical action that requires movement of muscles and bones, and so, when we speak, the physical takes the lead. But when we are silent, the spiritual takes over.[4] Silence thus both builds and *reveals* our inner world and the infinite spiritual treasures that lie within us.

"Some silence means cessation of speech," writes Rabbi Avraham Yitzchok Kook. "Another silence means cessation of thought. That silence arrives together with the most hidden, beautiful and exalted thought."[5] Those are the thoughts that my Mussar teacher, Rabbi Perr, says come from Heaven, and they come only to a silent mind. Shimon ben Gamliel summed up the importance of what we can gain from conversing less: "All my days have I grown up among the wise and I have not found anything better for a person than silence."[6]

Conversation connects us to other people, and, in the modern world, that connection is unceasing. By never interrupting the flow of banter, we not only never open ourselves to receive the gifts of silence, we lose the ability to be alone with ourselves. Many people maintain the endless stream of chatter for the simple reason that they have real discomfort at being alone and quiet. This comes with a cost.

The Mussar great of the last generation Rabbi Shlomo Wolbe writes,[7]

You can only get a feeling for your internal life when you are alone. With a half hour of being alone you can come to feel things you never knew about yourself and see what you are lacking in spirituality. You will set new goals to reach. This can only be done if you spend time alone in seclusion [*hitbodedut*] for half an hour. In this way you can start to build your internal, spiritual world.

Silence and solitude are precious, but so is speech; our challenge is to find the point of balance between the two. The answer is to speak succinctly, with clear and measured words, and no more. Rabbinic insight and even legal ruling often emerge from a single word or phrase and a nuance of how it is used. It is obvious that one must train oneself to be sensitive to how one's words can hurt and destroy, or build and heal. But even aside from the impact, being attuned to every word and shade of meaning you birth into the world honors the Creator and the created, as well as the gift of speech you have been given.

We are not guided to cut out the small talk entirely, because then we would lose the value of casual conversation. The call is to *limit* the chatter we emit, because a little is all that is needed. Even valuable talk needs to be limited. Rambam says that one should minimize speech even in matters of Torah and wisdom and expand one's thoughts.[8]

It is worth reflecting on your own willingness to shoot the breeze. Why do you do it? Is there some reward you are after? Does nattering deliver a real benefit? Can you identify where small talk is useful in your life, and where you might well cut back on the chatter?

The point of this whole lesson is to underline that speech is a precious faculty, and it is up to us to use it in a disciplined and restrained way. That's how we can ensure that its scope and power are applied only for the good, within you and in the world.

PRACTICE

The Mussar teachers have long advocated the practice of *hit-bodedut* (solitude). The Novarodokers took this to an extreme, starting with the Alter himself and his practice of spending extended periods secluded in a hut in the woods. Rav Wolbe and others take a softer approach by simply advocating time spent by oneself, taking walks and such.

Your practice for this period is to make for yourself a time of silence of at least ten minutes during the day. Carve out that time just to pursue reflective thought or quiet contemplation, in utter silence.

מיעוט סחורה

[17]

Limiting Work or Business

Miyut Sechorah

Earlier generations made the study of Torah their main concern
and their livelihood secondary and both prospered. Later generations made livelihood their main concern and Torah study
secondary and neither prospered.

—BERACHOT 35B

I T IS AN ongoing challenge to achieve the right balance between work and other activities. Half of the population seems
overburdened with an impossible workload, while the other half
are either unemployed or working below their education, experience, and need. Where lies the ideal to which we should aspire?

While many people profess to dislike working, engaging in
a working life can be very compelling, even addictive. Work
and all it entails can become an all-consuming preoccupation.
There are jobs whose demands are so extreme that a workweek
of sixty hours or more is the norm.

Greed may be an obvious motivator, but it certainly is not
the only factor that can cause a person to become overly in-

volved in his or her livelihood activities. Insecurity or fear can motivate the same behavior. Work can also give us the feeling of being productive and accomplished as we actualize the creative potential that resonates deep within our essential being. We can draw our very identity and our sense of value from the work we do.

Wealth, power, prestige, and even the satisfaction of accomplishment can all play a role in drawing a person into a lifestyle that centers on work, in which there is little time or energy or even interest for anything besides work.

The guidance we receive here is to set a limit on how much time and energy we give to making a living, and that ruling is explained more fully in a teaching from *Pirkei Avot* 4:9, in which Rabbi Meir says, "Minimize your business activities and occupy yourself with Torah." Here we learn *why* we are supposed to cut back on our worldly endeavors—not so we can spend more time sipping Pink Ladies at the nineteenth hole, but to free up our time for spiritual education and growth. When we allow work to take over our lives, it is almost impossible to pursue the spiritual goals that are our truest purpose for living.

The Chafetz Chaim again provides us with a role model. His family was supported by a store that was operated principally by his wife. The store became very successful, so the rabbi reduced the hours it was open to half the day.[1] That was enough.

The Chafetz Chaim supported his family with a store in keeping with another verse in *Pirkei Avot,* 4:7, where we are given another important thread to weave into our thinking here. Rabbi Tzadok taught, "Do not make the Torah a spade with which to dig," by which he meant make a living. Even though our spiritual lives ought to be our priority, we are still supposed to work in mundane ways for our income. And so it was that all of the Talmudic rabbis had jobs. Hillel was a woodchopper and Shammai a builder. Abba Chilkiyah was a field laborer; Rabbi Yochanan ben Zakkai was a businessman; Abba Shaul dug graves. Others of the great sages were launderers, cotton dealers, tanners, blacksmiths, tailors, vintners, farmers, and brewers. Shmuel (like the Rambam in a later generation) was a doctor. One classic rabbinic source sums it up: "A person should love work and not hate it; for just as the Torah was given with a covenant, so too was work given with a covenant."[2] But we need to limit our time spent working, so that it doesn't squeeze every other important activity out of our lives.

The tradition points us toward engaging in a profession or trade to earn our money, but how much of our time ought to be devoted to work pursuits? In the Talmud, some rabbis are praised because they "devoted one-third of their day to Torah, one-third to prayer and one-third to work. Others say that they toiled in Torah in the winter and at their work in the summer."[3]

The real challenge this particular method of spiritual transformation throws at us is to seek balance in our lives, which means that we have to practice moderation. The underlying requirement is nothing less than that we be the master of our desires and emotions. The world of business and money, income and bills, is fraught with a very compelling energy because it stimulates greed, involves our egos, and plays to our fears about survival. It is very easy to see how we get driven to work too much and too hard, even in seeking work, and to neglect the higher purpose of our lives.

A general principle of Jewish spiritual practice applies here. That guideline is to show restraint in things that we not only enjoy but tend to enjoy to excess. This was the contribution to our understanding of holiness made by the Ramban (also known as Nahmanides; 1194–c.1270). He said that holiness couldn't be just a matter of staying away from defiling influences because it is entirely possible to indulge in permissible things in ways that are surely not holy, like a person drinking kosher wine to the point of stupefaction or eating kosher food like a glutton. He called this "being a rascal with the permission of the Torah,"[4] and his teaching was that a spiritual seeker must certainly stay away from defilement, and then go beyond that by showing restraint in relation to permitted things.

Work can be a necessity and even a covenantal virtue, but if our days are so occupied with it that we have no time and energy to engage in the things that are the soul's highest priorities, then we need to take steps to limit how much we work.

In *Pirkei Avot* 2:5 we are advised, "Don't say, 'When I'm free I will study,' for perhaps you will never be free." Rambam quotes this cautionary teaching and explains that there is something inherently problematic in the mindset that says, "When I have enough money, I'll study" or "When I have accumulated enough of the possessions I want, then I'll be ready to commit to my spiritual life."[5] The problem is priorities! What are your priorities? Right now.

Many sources sing the same tune, loudly: Make an honest assessment of what you really need, and engage in your work to achieve that level and no more. Then you will be free to attain what you want. The rabbis caution us that getting too involved with our mundane pursuits will keep us from our spiritual ones. Commenting on the verse in the Torah, "It is not across the seas" (Deuteronomy 30:13), they say clearly, "Torah does not reside with those who cross the seas for business" (Eruvin 55a). The essential point they are driving at is made specific in *Pirkei Avot* (2:6): "One who engages excessively in business cannot become wise."[6]

PRACTICE

On a piece of paper, or in your journal, make a list of the reasons you work.

Now make a separate list of the highest aspirations you have for your life.

Reflect on the ways and extent to which your reasons for working dovetail with the larger goals you have set for your life. Is there a good fit, or do you see discrepancy?

If any discrepancy has shown up, resolve to adjust your work life to be subservient to your spiritual goals by limiting the amount of time and energy you give to work or business activities.

מיעוט שחוק

[18]

Limiting Levity

Miyut S'chok

The tongue of the wise commends knowledge, but the mouths
of fools pour out folly.

—PROVERBS 15:2

WHAT'S THE problem with laughter? Nothing, really. The
Talmud contains many funny comments, though when
someone once asked Rabbi Aryeh Kaplan whether there were
jokes in the Talmud, he answered, "Yes, but they are all old."
We're told that the great sage Rabbah always began his lectures
with a funny comment.[1] How many great Jewish comedians
have there been, and how many great Jewish jokes?

The Talmud even goes so far as to single out comedians for
eternal reward.[2] Rabbi Beroka was once in the marketplace
when the prophet Elijah came to him. The rabbi asked, "Is there
anyone in this marketplace who will find a place in the World-
to-Come?" Elijah answered, "No." Just then, two men walked
by, and Elijah told the rabbi, "These men deserve a place in the
World-to-Come." Rabbi Beroka went to them and asked their

occupation. "We are comedians," they told him, "and we cheer up those who are depressed. In addition, whenever we see two people involved in quarrel, we work hard to make peace between them."

There are even Mussar jokes. A new student comes to a Novarodok yeshiva and during the first Mussar session begins to beat his chest and cry out in humility, "I am nothing! I am nothing!" An older student nudges his friend and whispers, "Look who's been here for one day and already thinks he's nothing!" My Mussar teacher, Rabbi Perr, says that a good Mussar talk contains both tears and laughter.

There is a place for humor in spiritual life, but not all humor is the same. In pointing out the need to limit laughter, the Mishnah is alerting us to two different issues. One is about insensitive humor. The other is about silly, excessive laughter.

We've all heard jokes that make us laugh and cringe at the same time. Ridicule or mockery, for example, can be very funny but always at someone else's expense. We see the same thing with jokes that demean, such as ethnic, racial, and sexist jokes. It can't be good for the soul to find enjoyment while hurting someone else in any way, including with humor. And if you are the one at the butt end of such humor, you know how bad it feels. Did you hear the one about the Jew who . . . ?

Mockery is roundly condemned in the tradition. The Talmud lists four groups who will not receive the Divine Presence, one of which is mockers.[3] Proverbs 24:9 calls one who mocks "an abomination." The Mussar teacher Rabbi Moshe Chaim Luzzatto cautions us strongly about "the power of mockery, which obliterates all facets of Mussar and *yirah*,"[4] which literally means the awe, reverence, and fear of the Creator and stands for the core of spiritual living. Mockery comes from and breeds cynicism, which is the antithesis of the sensitive and caring heart we seek.

If we pay attention, we will see that whenever we experience abusive humor, we feel empty and a bit sick afterward.

The other issue is a tendency to indulge in excessive laughter. We've all been in the room with someone who laughs too much, too long, too loud. That sort of laughter appears foolish and is experienced as a kind of assault. There is desperation in indulging in so much mirth, a visceral wish that life would be other than it is. And while I fully endorse my friend Wavy Gravy's motto that without a sense of humor, life just isn't funny anymore, at the same time, life is not to be wasted, and excessive frivolity undermines the meaning and depth that are the richness of life.

Humor can be a safety valve for the pressures of life. It releases the tension that comes from living within restrictive boundaries. The setup for a joke acknowledges that tension ("A priest, a minister, and a rabbi debate, 'When does life begin?'"), and then the punch line releases us from that tension ("When the kids move out and the dog dies"). Without a setup to build tension, there will be no release, and if the release is delayed, the tension will already have dissipated.

So is release from the strict parameters and the inevitable tensions of our lives a good thing? Why would we want to escape the rigorous discipline that study and spiritual growth demand? The answer, it appears, is that a little is beneficial, while too much is dangerous. As with all our innate human drives and capacities, the Mussar approach is not to repress or deny but to contain and direct, so the drive is used for a holy purpose. The release brought on by laughter can be good, but the test lies in controlling it, binding it, so that it doesn't become our way of life.

Could that be one of the messages we are meant to take from the story of the *binding* of Yitzchak,[5] in light of the fact that the very name "Yitzchak" means "he will laugh"?[6]

The release afforded by humor is built into the ritual observance of the Jewish festival of Purim. In many yeshivot, one of the sharp-witted students is appointed "Purim Rabbi." He takes his place at the head of the table and delivers a Talmudic lecture imitating and poking fun at the rosh yeshiva and rabbis. Throughout the year, the students experience the pressures of living within the strictures imposed by their teachers, and all that tension is relieved with humor on Purim. Rav Avraham Yitzchok Kook once had this role at the Volozhin Yeshiva, where he delivered the talk not in the usual Yiddish but in Hebrew and Aramaic. Try being funny in Aramaic.

The caution is that release from boundaries has become a way of life in modern society. Public behavior that was unthinkable only one generation back is now the norm, and the media glory in the antics of every egotist who shows up on reality television to parade his or her further debasement of public standards. Media careers are built on gossip and negative speech. The highest-grossing films are the ones that celebrate and deliver the most thoroughgoing escapism.

Humor works well in spiritual life when it is a pinch of spice added to the main course of serious endeavor. It relaxes the mind and refreshes the energy that we need to continue to study and to grow. But, like all spice, it tastes best when used only in moderation.

The sensitive soul recognizes the truth we find in Ecclesiastes 3:4: "There is a time to weep and a time to laugh, a time to mourn and a time to dance," and the sensitivity comes in knowing which is which, and how to respond in a whole and holy way that is appropriate to the situation.

PRACTICE

Because humor satisfies us on a deep psychological level, we can often be unconscious of how and when we put its power to use. Your practice, then, is to try to be aware of when you call on humor in your interactions with others.

As you observe yourself being drawn to make a funny comment, tell a joke, quip or be witty, pay attention to the tension you are trying to dissipate through your use of humor.

From where does that tension emanate—from you, the other person, or the interaction? What is it about that tension that makes you feel motivated to dissipate it? What would it look like to meet that tension head-on, to dissipate it in another way besides humor?

And what about how you laugh? Be on the lookout for excessive laughter.

These questions and others like them that may apply to you are perfect for addressing in your Mussar journal because it is difficult to achieve depth of understanding in the midst of a tense situation and much easier to probe and understand in retrospect.

[19]

Limiting Pleasure

Miyut Ta'anug

He who loves pleasure will become poor; whoever loves wine
and oil will never be rich.

—PROVERBS 21:17

JUDAISM is not at all opposed to pleasure. We have no tradition of monasticism or celibacy or much of an ascetic tradition. Self-denial is generally limited in scope and application, which is part of what makes Yom Kippur stand out on the calendar. The Jerusalem Talmud even says, "On Judgment Day, a person will be called to account for every permissible thing he might have enjoyed in life but did not."[1]

If there is no objection to pleasure, why the caution to limit it? The answer is that when we are heavily involved in seeking pleasure, the physical inevitably supplants the spiritual as the guiding principle in our lives. The Jewish way is to enjoy the pleasures of the world within the context of a spiritual life. That way of living requires that we be the masters of our sensory pleasures, rather than having them rule over us.

It's so easy to lose ourselves in a bag of potato chips or a chocolate bar and more so in more intense forms of physical sensation. Not only lose ourselves, but become devotees of the perfect cup of coffee, the smokiness of a single-malt scotch, the thread count of organic cotton sheets. We are being asked to be conscious and make wise choices about where we direct our desire for pleasure and to be careful that we not allow physical pleasures to occupy the center of our lives.

The Maharal explains that the more one indulges the body, the more bodily one becomes, and that impedes connection to the spiritual.[2] The Talmud tells of Rav Kahana sitting in front of his teacher, Rav, and fixing his hair and pampering himself, whereupon Rav castigated him, saying, "The Torah is not found in one who indulges physically."[3]

Rabbi Yerucham Levovitz asked why the Torah was given in the inhospitable desert.[4] Why not give it once we had made it across the Jordan to the Promised Land, where people could embrace the Torah with settled minds? He explains that having inner calmness does, indeed, facilitate acquiring Torah, but people mistakenly think that indulging the body is the way to achieve that inner settledness. The truth is that the more one indulges the body, the more comforts we become accustomed to, the more dependent we become on these things, and the *harder* it becomes to maintain a calm frame of mind.

Rabbi Yerucham compares a person who tries to settle the mind by indulging the body to a thirsty person who drinks salt water, or one who throws oil on a fire that he wants to extinguish. For a brief moment it seems that the goal has been accomplished, but then the thirst comes back even stronger or the fire rages out of control. The desert was the perfect place to receive the Torah because the desert is a place of *limited physical pleasures.* If you are less attached to gratification, external circumstances will have less power to throw you off the inner calmness that is so necessary for spiritual growth.

We find this idea echoed in another teaching of the Maharal. He asks why *matzah* is the symbol of freedom on Passover? He answers that *matzah* is made of only flour and water, just the bare necessities and no more. The more one establishes physical needs, the more a slave one becomes, but if one can subsist on the bare necessities, one can be truly free.

We should not be more involved in the physical than we need to be. And where we do seek pleasure, it should never be an end in itself. Any experience of pleasure can be "lifted" to a higher level. A delicious flavor, a beautiful sight, or a fine sensation can and should be an inspiration for awe and awareness of the Divine. This is a teaching of the Slonimer Rebbe,[5] who invokes Jacob's dream to teach that whereas Jacob's ladder "stands on the earth" (the starting point is our earthiness), nevertheless its "head reaches up to heaven."[6] He teaches that "when a person follows the Divine Will and raises this attribute to its source, he reaches up to heaven."[7]

The Slonimer understands that having desires is an inescapable aspect of being human, but he guides us to become the stewards of those desires so that they are sources of elevation, not debasement. "The quality of yearning is one that completely encompasses a person; it begins in the recesses of the mind, and continues through one's emotions and one's actions. A person's spiritual state is wholly dependent on the nature of his yearnings. The holy Torah phrases the commandment [to be holy] in the positive for this reason. The commandment is to direct one's yearning toward the holy—toward the Blessed One, toward delight in God, toward pleasure in the radiance of the Divine Presence."[8]

Indeed, the entire universe exists for the sake of our pleasure. This is the remarkable opening teaching in that pillar of Mussar *Path of the Just*. In it Rabbi Luzzatto acknowledges that we are creatures of pleasure and the pursuit of pleasure is our purpose, but the test in life is to choose spiritual pleasure over physical gratification. "Our Sages of blessed memory have taught us that man was created for the sole purpose of rejoicing in God and deriving pleasure from the splendor of His Presence; for this is true joy and the greatest pleasure that can be found."[9]

In line with this concept, Rabbi Shlomo Wolbe agrees with Freud that pleasure is the determining factor behind all of our actions. Where he differs, however, is in seeing the true pleasure as spiritual and the ultimate pleasure as being close to God. Physical and earthly pleasures offer a faint shadow of this truest pleasure, and a person who settles for that level of fulfillment has exchanged the real thing for a poor substitute, trading living waters for cracked cisterns.[10] The question is only what gives a person pleasure—"Tell me what you enjoy and I will tell you who you are!"[11]

At the core, each of us is a holy soul, but this truth is hidden and elusive. The more we give ourselves over to the captivating pleasures of the tongue and skin, the more our soul-nature is obscured. Then we forget who we are, and we lose sight of the spiritual journey we are on. Moderate your investment in pleasure and earn a spiritual dividend. Reawaken the awareness of your spiritual nature, using your physical desires to ring the wake-up bell.

PRACTICE

There must be many things you do in your day that you enjoy. In fact, if you take a good look, you may have to admit that you organize your hours around various pleasures, be it a morning coffee (and perhaps not *just* a coffee, but a specific blend with certain ingredients prepared a certain way) or a particular lunch you enjoy, or perhaps it is someone you count on speaking to every day, or a television show you watch.

Make note of what you do in your day that you enjoy. Then determine how you could limit that pleasure without eliminating it altogether. How can you "tone it down" in such a way as to reduce your attachment to what the physical delivers to you?

If you think you can't cut back like that, you will discover that you can. When you try, you will see how strong are the attachments to pleasure that bind you to your habitual indulgences. Let that insight be a motivator to pursue the spiritual more than the physical.

מיעוט דרך ארץ

[20]

Limiting Mundane Activities

Miyut Derekh Eretz

Let all your deeds be for the sake of heaven.

—*PIRKEI AVOT* 2:12

*D*EREKH ERETZ is a phrase that literally means "the way of the land." It is often used to refer to the sorts of mundane or worldly activities we do because of work obligations, social expectations, or etiquette. We are cautioned to restrain our engagement with those sorts of activities because they can conflict with or pull against our spiritual practice. Limiting how much time and investment we make in mundane everyday activities means doing what the world requires of us, but only to the minimum, and no more.

Though we are guided to limit mundane activities, acting with *derekh eretz* is nevertheless considered to be a positive thing to do. For example, it is considered polite and decent for a young person to stand when an older person or a teacher enters the room. It is a matter of *derekh eretz* that we are expected to work to make a living. And while no legislation dictates how one must answer the telephone, saying "What?" in place of "Hello" clearly shows a lack of *derekh eretz*.

So important is correct social behavior that we are told, "*Derekh eretz* preceded the Torah by 26 generations."[1] That would date good behavior to the time of Adam and Eve, and it continued to be valued in every generation until the Torah was received by Moses and the laws of human behavior were codified. There is something essential about living in accordance with social conventions because, in reality, society can only exist when we do that.

The stress on honoring social obligations is a corollary of the fact that Jewish spiritual practice calls on us to engage our curriculum of growth nowhere other than in the everyday world of family, work, friends, and the marketplace—not in an artificial oasis of solitude and withdrawal. Making the everyday world the locus of spiritual practice challenges us to figure out how to foster our souls in the midst of all that goes on in the world. Practicing *derekh eretz* is part of that equation.

With just that reality in mind, the Mussar teacher the Alter of Slobodka[2] encouraged the students in his nineteenth-century yeshiva to dress like middle-class European businessmen, with a neat and clean hat and jacket, pressed trousers, and a waistcoat. He saw this as spiritual practice. Dressing and conducting oneself with worldly dignity were intended to lead to a refinement of character and an internalizing of the sense of the greatness of a human being[3] that was his primary teaching.

Discerning when to say, "When in Rome, do as the Romans do," and when it is right to show unbending stubbornness in pursuing your own personal curriculum of growth and finding the balance between these dual obligations are difficult challenges faced by the spiritually sensitive person who engages with the modern world. Wisdom and awareness, as well as clarity about your own convictions, will serve you better than any hard-and-fast rules. Indeed, it is acknowledged that "there is no wisdom like the wisdom of *derekh eretz.*"[4] One thing is certain: Sometimes personal growth demands that we *limit* our engagement with the general ways the people around us behave.

For example, we all know that time is precious, yet every generation has found ways to waste time. Our current generation has taken this practice to new heights. The Internet can be very useful, but it also has the potential to be a bottomless chasm into which entire days and weeks can be poured. Special vessels for wasting time have been invented—starting with social media websites but including many other sorts of Internet sites, from the relatively benign (like solitaire and sudoku) to the clearly harmful (such as pornography and, only to a slightly lesser degree, celebrity gossip).

More amazing, perhaps, is that the world at large puts a positive value on wasting time. Secular culture celebrates unfettered freedom—what the philosophers call "freedom from." Individual liberty is highly valued, and wasting time is a clear indicator that a person owes fealty to no one. I am a free person, and if I want to sit on a cruise ship and eat five meals a day while traveling between nearly identical tourist ports that I can't name, no one can stop me. But is that what life is for?

In contrast, Judaism celebrates "freedom *to,*" under which a person freely engages in commitments and embraces constraints that serve a higher purpose. When you align to a higher purpose, wasting time is anathema. The implication is that time is very valuable, and, indeed, there is a concept in Judaism that teaches this notion. *Yakrut ha'zman* refers to the preciousness of time.

A famous story about Rabbi Yisrael Salanter tells of him

walking by the shop of a shoemaker who was working by the light of a candle. When Rav Yisrael asked the man why he was still working so late into the night, the man answered, "As long as the candle is still burning, there is time to repair." The *neshama*-soul is likened to a candle,[5] and Rabbi Salanter taught from this experience that as long as the soul is still illuminated, we have the opportunity to purify and elevate our inner beings, to develop in the direction of holiness and wholeness. There is no time to waste.

The core of the issue is revealed by asking yourself, Which master do I serve? In the modern world, many masters vie for our allegiance. Some people serve the deities of the popular media and orient their lives according to current trends and fashions. Others are totally committed to their work or career. Gangs and family and sports teams claim the faithfulness of some, while there are those who would do anything to win popular approval, just to belong. There are deep human needs and drives at work here.

In contrast, we read in *Pirkei Avot* 5:23, "Be bold as a leopard . . . to carry out the will of your Father in Heaven." This is where the Jewish spiritual seeker is meant to affix primary allegiance. Sometimes we have to bend this way or that just to make life work according to the ways of the world in which we live, but we need to affirm and reaffirm and internalize that we have a primary commitment and, in consequence, minimize any other. It is not a mere turn of phrase that the two initial leaders of the Jewish people, Moses and Joshua, are both referred to as "servants of God."[6]

The candle is still burning, but it won't stay lit forever. Time is precious. Will you reach your goals?

PRACTICE

In the final words that the Torah gives us to describe Moses, we read, "And Moses, the servant of God, died."[7] This could be taken to be Moses's obituary. When all was said and done and his life needed to be summed up, the Torah tells us that the essential thing we should know about him was that he was a servant of God.

When the time comes that someone will write your obituary, what will it say about whom you served?

I invite you to answer this question by writing a paragraph that summarizes the priorities that have dominated your life to this point. That's another way of saying whom or what you have served. Be honest.

Having that truth in writing is the basis for the next step, which is now to sketch in writing the highest purposes you would like to serve in your life. Identifying and underlining those high purposes will help bring into focus what you need to do to reach that way of living—limit the time you give to anything that is not a high priority. That is your practice for this period.

אֶרֶךְ אַפַּיִם

[21]

Slow to Anger

Erech Apayim

Better to be slow to anger than mighty, to have self-control
than conquer a city.

—PROVERBS 16:32

ADONAI, ADONAI! Compassionate and gracious, slow to
anger, abounding in kindness and faithfulness . . ." we
intone on festival days and especially on Yom Kippur.[1] Notice
that the quality of being slow to anger figures highly on the list
of characteristics that are ascribed to God.

"God's anger" is a metaphor for the divine response to transgressive human behavior. This gives us a model we can apply in
our own lives to guide how we respond when we are provoked
by someone else's behavior. To be slow to anger is to be tolerant
or, in another phrase, long suffering.

The phrase *erech apayim* literally means "long of nose." What
does that have to do with anger? It means that when someone is
provoked (and that someone could be God) and before they
react they take a long breath, their response in anger is delayed. The longer the nose, the longer the breath, the more time

there is for another response, like compassion and understanding, to take the place of anger.

We all get angry, we all know that most of the time we shouldn't, and we all need to be reminded that we have the capacity to choose other responses that will carry us more in the direction of holiness than will anger.

God provides the role model of being slow to anger, and Rabbi Moshe Cordovero, a prominent kabbalist and Mussar teacher of the sixteenth century, provides a clear description of how we know this to be the case, writing,[2]

> There is no moment when a person is not nourished and does not exist except by virtue of the divine power that flows down upon him. It follows that no one ever sins against God without the divine outpouring flowing into him at that very moment, enabling him to exist and to move his limbs. Despite the fact that he uses it for sin, that power is not withheld from him in any way. Instead, the Holy One, Blessed be He, bears this insult and continues to empower him to move his limbs even though he uses the power in that moment for sin and perversity offending the Holy One, Blessed is He, who, nonetheless, suffers it.

Since one of the primary guidelines of Mussar is to model our behavior on what we know of God's ways,[3] it follows that if God is slow to respond angrily to provocation, then we, too, should strive to delay our reactions. As the verse says, "At a time of anger God reminds Himself of His mercy."[4] By breathing deeply and not jumping to react, we open a space in which to remind ourselves that we have the capacity to choose another response in place of our anger.

Being slow to anger does not mean that a person should accept being a victim, but neither is there great virtue in acting out one's anger even in responding to injustice. In fact, reactivity is an instinctive characteristic of animals, and what distinguishes humans from other animals is our ability to override emotions with wisdom. Rabbi Perr speaks of Mussar practice helping to open "a space between the match and the fuse," which could be a definition of wisdom itself. Being slow to react affords us a better perspective from which to respond.

A story is told about a Chassidic leader who would dispense "holy water" guaranteed to eliminate all domestic conflicts. Whenever a husband or wife had an urge to argue, he or she was to hold some of the water in his or her mouth without swallowing for as long as possible. This "holy water" proved to be very effective in stopping arguments and diffusing anger. Similarly, the Alter of Kelm made a personal resolution never to get angry unless he first put on a special garment he had set aside as his "anger clothes."

Jewish sources relate anger to foolishness ("For anger lingers in the bosom of fools")[5] and to loss of wisdom ("One who becomes angry, if he is wise, his wisdom leaves him")[6]—and really these are just two sides of the same coin. How does someone in a rage look to you? Wise? How do you think you appear to others when you act out of anger? Perhaps foolish? Indeed, anger is more often than not an ineffective or even counterproductive tactic, and only a fool willingly does something that is counterproductive.[7]

The sages recognized that what lies at the root of anger is often exaggerated pride or self-centeredness. It is said that anger is akin to idol worship.[8] The "false god" referred to in this teaching is the god of self-worship. The bigger the ego, the more easily one is moved to anger. Rabbi Yisrael Salanter reflected on a story in the Talmud about a man who was insulted by his wife and then went to sleep in a cemetery.[9] Rabbi Salanter explained that the man did so with the intention of breaking the pride that was prompting him to respond with anger.

Learning from God, we don't want to rush to righteous judgment, because that doesn't create a space in which the other person has the opportunity to correct what they have done to offend us. How much better to receive an apology that can heal a rift than to deliver a blow (even if only verbal) that deepens one.

Another very good reason to be slow to anger is that you may not have your facts right. I was once waiting for my bags in an airport and overheard a woman berating someone over the phone for not being there to pick her up. After a stream of invective came a pause, and then, "You mean there's a time difference?"

You have to wonder, too, if getting angry is the most skillful and effective response you can come up with. Since I mention airports, I was once in line at customer service because the airline had messed up and I missed my flight. I had every right to be annoyed, and I was. The line was long, however, and, as I was forced to wait, I had time to cool down enough to realize that if I unleashed my righteous anger, it would feel very good in that moment, but almost certainly I'd be paying for my own hotel room that night. If I could smooth out that anger and respond from a different place, there was a chance the airline would pay for my room. How much better to be an effective victor than a self-gratified loser.

Here we have three good reasons to be slow to anger. And there are more, too. In fact, it is hard to think of a single reason to praise being quick to anger.

PRACTICE

Being slow to anger requires that you be patient and tolerant. The Hebrew word for patience is *savlanut,* which comes from the same root as "suffer" (*sevel*) and "porter" (*sabal*). Being patient means bearing or carrying your own emotional suffering. In practice, that means becoming aware of difficult emotions as you experience them, and then just holding them, even embracing them, so they do not take you over and dictate your behavior. You still respond, but it is *you* responding, not just the passion of the moment roaring through you. That's real patience, and that is what you are assigned for this period.

Everything that builds awareness contributes to introducing the space between the match and the fuse, including keeping a journal, meditating, praying, reading Mussar books, and so on. In particular, for this period, your assignment is to practice the Mussar method found in many places that advises living out in your mind's eye a potentially provocative situation before it occurs.

If you anticipate that you are going to find yourself in a situation that might get heated, try to imagine in advance the argument that might take place. Then, should the hot words actually start to fly, instead of shooting back from shock and affront, your experience will be one of recognition: "This is what I prepared for." That very thought will help pry open the space between the match and the fuse, that precious territory within which free will and wisdom reside.

לב טוב

[22]

Goodheartedness

Lev Tov

Rabban Yochanan ben Zakkai said to them: "Go and see which
is the good a person should cherish most." Rabbi Eliezer said a
good eye. Rabbi Yehoshua said a good companion. Rabbi Yosi
said a good neighbor. Rabbi Shimon said foresight. Rabbi Elazar said a good heart. He said to them, "I prefer the words of
Elazar ben Arach for his words include yours."

—PIRKEI AVOT 2:13

WHEN THE Rogatchover Gaon was a young man,[1] he
met with the great Rabbi Tzadok HaKohen of Lublin
(1823–1900). They discussed deep topics, and as the Rogatchover prepared to depart, Reb Tzadok told him, "You are perhaps
the greatest genius in the new generation. I was also a prodigy
but I eventually learned that though scholarship is wonderful,
real greatness lies in a *lev tov*." The younger man reported that
this statement changed his life.

What does it mean to have a *lev tov*, a good heart?

A good heart sees the good in others. A good heart smiles
easily. A good heart opens up to the heart of another. A good

heart is able to bond with another good heart and to bring that person close.

Rabbeinu Yonah of Gerona refines our understanding by saying that a good heart is especially adept at being patient. Some explain that the quality of a good heart follows right after our previous lesson on being slow to anger to illustrate that there is a relationship between these two qualities.[2] A person who is tolerant and patient draws those behaviors from the internal well of a *lev tov*.

But there are other interpretations, as well. Rabbi Samson Raphael Hirsch (1808–88)[3] offers, "A person who has a good heart is one in whom envy, jealousy and hate can gain no access."[4] The Maharal of Prague finds different qualities in the good heart: "a soft nature and the ability to act joyfully for the benefit of others."[5]

But are these views really that different? Resisting envy is not the same as acting joyfully for the benefit of others, which differs again from exercising patience, of course, but taking a larger view, a good heart can be seen to be one that is not selfish, not overly concerned with its own benefit, and much more oriented to the well-being of others than to its own satisfactions. Concern for the other both reflects and cultivates a good heart.

Much of Jewish practice is bound up with codes and behaviors, asking that we pay close attention to the details of performances. With the concern for the good heart, we are being reminded to pay attention to the inner experience that lies behind the action. Many teachers in many contexts have underlined the adage that "God desires the heart,"[6] because it is not enough just to do the right thing. As the early nineteenth-century Mussar teacher Rabbi Eliezer Papo writes, "All of Judaism and the service of God depend upon a good heart."[7]

For example, Judaism commands that we give charity, but is

the act of giving, even if very generously, enough? No, the quality of the heart that motivates the gift is so important that one primary source tells us, "Even if a person gives someone the most precious gifts in the world but his face is gloomy, then it is as if he gave nothing. But one who greets his friend with a pleasant countenance is considered to have given the best gifts in the world, even if he did not actually give any gifts at all."[8]

Indeed, the code of Jewish law, the *Shulchan Aruch,* rules explicitly, "One must give charity with a pleasant countenance, with joy and with a good heart, empathizing with the plight of the poor person and offering words of comfort. If one gives with a sad face then the benefit of giving is lost."[9]

We shouldn't be satisfied to do just what is expected of us; we should do those actions with qualities of the heart that match our outer goodness. In the words of the rabbis, "The inside should be like the outside."[10] How much more do we need a good heart to guide us when we find ourselves in circumstances that call on us to go beyond what is required of us or to do something that is actually not required at all?

Take, for example, the situation that confronted Moses when it was he and not his elder brother, Aharon, who was chosen to lead the people of Israel. Moses worried that Aharon would be hurt because he had been passed over for the leadership, but God reassured him, saying, "Behold, he [Aharon] is going out to meet you and when he sees you, he will rejoice in his heart."[11] The situation had to be difficult for Aharon, but because he had—and had actually cultivated—a *lev tov,* he yearned for the joy and success of others, and that inner attitude extended to celebrating the leadership role that had been assigned to his own younger brother.[12]

The wonderful Yiddish word *fargen* captures this quality. The undeveloped heart tends to slide into resentment and envy at another's good fortune. The Yiddish writer Sholom Aleichem captured this perfectly by saying that when he had a good day at the market, he told his friends that he had a bad day. That way, he was happy and they were happy. But if he had a bad day, he told his friends that he had a good day, because that way, his misery had company. But the good heart doesn't fall into that common pattern that Sholom Aleichem describes so well. The goodhearted person *fargens,* which means that he or she rejoices in another person's happiness and good fortune.

And just as much, the goodhearted person feels another person's sorrow. Rabbi Yitzchok Elchonon Spector (1817–96) was an important legal authority in his generation.[13] He was once approached by an *agunah* (a woman who is considered to be in "chains" because her husband cannot or will not provide a divorce document) who was seeking release from her marriage.

After much effort, Rav Yitzchok Elchonon failed to find a legal basis that justified granting her wish. Upon hearing this news, the woman burst into bitter tears. Rav Yitzchok Elchonon heard, saw, and felt her tears and dove back into the legal precedents with even more effort and determination. In the end, he came up with an eight-page response that permitted freeing the woman from her marriage. His *lev tov* guided him to many innovations in Torah interpretation that he had not seen before.

The Vilna Gaon points out that rain causes whatever is in the earth to grow, whether food or flowers or noxious weeds.[14] Similarly, our Torah study and spiritual practice serve to "water" whatever is seeded in the heart—if good, it will cause the good to grow, but if one is saddled with negative *middot,* like seeking honor or being selfish or self-righteous, then those tendencies will be caused to flourish. We need to be concerned about the quality of our heart, because everything we do in our lives will be an outgrowth of what it is that we have planted there. As is well known, good intentions are not enough to save us from the reality of what lives in our hearts.

When Rabbi Yochanan Ben Zakai (c.30–90 C.E.) asked his students to define the best path a person ought to follow in life, he approved of the answer, "a good heart."[15] We need to cultivate a good heart in order to merit the transformation that we call acquiring Torah.

PRACTICE

A story is told about the Vilna Gaon when he was still a young boy and already diligent in his Torah studies. The doctor told his mother that he needed to get outside and play more. She forced him to go to the park where the children were playing, but he soon returned home. When questioned, he explained that he could not take part in a game in which when one goes up, he causes the other to fall. The kids were playing on a seesaw. The young scholar already had such great sensitivity in his *lev tov,* sensitivity that allowed the Torah he studied to affect him so greatly.

Everyone knows not to kill or steal, but a person who aspires to holiness must be sensitive to the subtle nuances that show up in much less bold ways. As you go through your days in this period, be on the lookout for how your words and actions toward other people might have the effect of taking yourself "up" while easing the other person "down."

To be proactive, reach out to someone from your *lev tov.* Remember, care for the needs of the other reflects—and also nurtures—a good heart. Who needs something you are able to offer? Please make that offer, for the sake of the other and for the sake of your own good heart.

[23]

Faith in the Sages

Emunat Chachamim

Do not stray to the right or left from the word that they declare
to you.

—DEUTERONOMY 17:11

WHEN HE COMBED through the written Torah to identify
the 613 commandments that are the backbone of Jewish
practice, the Rambam recognized faith (*emunah*) as the very first
mitzvah.

The Brisker Rav, Rabbi Yitzchok Zev Soloveitchik (1887–
1959), once questioned his father and teacher because faith
seemed so self-evident to him. The existence of God was so
obvious and inescapable that he didn't understand what role
"faith" ought to play in life. His father answered that there are
things that the intellect can grasp and we call them "knowledge." Spiritual reality is beyond time and space, however, and
though we can sense, intuit, and even experience connection to
that ephemeral realm, it encompasses realities the intellect is
simply not equipped to grasp. Faith *begins* at the point where our

sure knowledge ceases. This principle applies to faith in God and also to faith in the sages of the tradition.

Who are the sages in whom we are supposed to have such faith? We have the written law (Torah), and then we have the oral law, which is the exposition of scripture that was committed to writing only after the destruction of the Temple and the beginning of exile. This is the Mishnah and the Talmud, as well as the many *midrashim* from that period. In the first instance, the oral law constitutes the work of the sages.[1]

The fact is, though, that the task of compiling the law did not stop when the Talmud was completed, around 500 C.E. In every generation we have had sages who have shouldered the task of knowing the Torah that has already been illuminated so well that they could apply it to the ever-changing situations of the human world. This process makes possible the development of new concepts and ideas that still represent Torah and are still the work of the sages, but that did not exist in the world previously.

In recent times, we have had to rely on sages because the Talmud did not contemplate electricity and airplanes or reproductive technologies that are commonplace today. The Jews escaping the Holocaust who sought refuge in Kobe, Japan, had no idea when to begin Shabbat because they were living on the far side of the International Date Line, a situation not imagined in the days of the Talmud. Until they consulted the sages of their time, some of them were observing Shabbat on Saturday and others on Sunday.

And what will happen if people leave this planet to live somewhere in space? When will they celebrate Passover on the moon or Yom Kippur on Mars? How do you establish the timing of the daily prayer services when your "day" is only two hours long?

We need to rely on the sages of our time to help guide us through the innumerable difficult issues that crop up that are unique to the modern world. The call to have faith in our sages is rooted in the verse that tells us, "Do not stray to the right or left from the word that they declare to you."[2] Rashi (Rabbi Shlomo Yitzhaki; 1040–1105) interprets this verse to mean further "even if they tell you your right is your left and your left is your right."[3]

On first glance, this sounds like we are being asked to have blind faith, but that cannot be. Rav Dessler explains that having faith in the sages does not mean that one can never question them or their rulings.[4] It is intrinsic to the Jewish way of spiritual growth that we question and argue. We have the right (and, in fact, the obligation!) to raise questions and to exercise our intellects. Our minds need to be firmly in gear in order that we can grasp the truths taught by our teachers.

But there are many ways to question. Because we enter the territory of faith when we reach the outer boundary of knowledge, the stance of having faith in the sages calls on us to assume that the wisest of people understand what we do not. The boundary of their knowledge extends beyond the measure of our own. When we question them, it is questioning based in humility, not to prove them wrong but to develop our own understanding and to come to a better grasp of truth, perhaps to push outward the boundary of our own knowledge.

The great sage of his time Rabbi Akiva Eiger was famous for finding seeming contradictions within earlier sources.[5] He often begins his investigation of a topic with "I have not merited to grasp the truth" or "I have not merited to understand his holy words." This is the best attitude to have when approaching the teachings of the sages. If we cannot grasp the wisdom that is before us, we must question, but even that seeming critique needs to be set within the context of faith. To grow in the way of Torah and to internalize its gifts, we are meant to question and probe constructively within a perspective that affirms the authenticity of the tradition transmitted to us through the sages.

Faith in the sages is justified because what qualifies an individual to the title of sage is not a college degree or even encyclopedic knowledge. The Hebrew word I have been translating as "sage" is *chachamim,* which literally means "wise ones." The sages are people in our tradition who have sought and gained extraordinary access to depths of Torah knowledge that they have then internalized and metabolized into wisdom. Some of the great sages of recent times, like the Chazon Ish,[6] were widely respected, even though they held no rabbinic post, led no yeshiva, and had no official title in the Jewish world. What people saw in them was wisdom.

Faith resides in the heart, and it is there that it must be cultivated and accessed. Perfect faith is achieved, not by philosophical inquiry, but by opening up and exposing the tender flesh of our hearts. The sages have extraordinary access to depths of Torah knowledge. That is the gift they bring to us and that we should open our hearts to receive and treasure.

PRACTICE

There is no doubt that human understanding of some things has advanced through the generations. We're better off basing medical decisions, for example, on science than on the teaching of the ancient sages. But when it comes to internalizing perennial wisdom, there has been no advance; and, if newspapers are any guide, a good argument can be made that there has been a "decline through the generations."[7]

Consider and reflect in your journal on this question:

In regard to acting with wisdom, on what basis would you trust anyone more than our sages—including yourself?

The emphasis in the question is on the *basis* for trust. In the case of medicine, that basis is science. In the case of wisdom for living, what basis or bases come into play?

Make that a serious inquiry. Ask yourself, "What criteria would I apply to determining whom more than our sages would I trust to be a source of wisdom and guidance for my life, and why?"

קבלת היסורין

[24]

Accepting Suffering

Kabbalat ha'Yissurin

How long, O Lord? Will you forget me forever? How long will
you hide Your face from me? How long must I bear pain in my
soul, and have sorrow in my heart all day long?

—PSALMS 13:1–2

WHAT CAN WE make of the suffering that exists in the
world when there seems to be no sense to it? Good people suffer, and people who do terrible wrong appear to enjoy the
best of what life has to offer. So many explanations have been
offered. Some tell us, "Our misfortunes are none of God's
doing," which certainly contradicts Jewish notions of divine
omnipotence. But does it work better to attribute cause to God,
as if God wants us to suffer? Today's method offers us an invitation to focus on our response to suffering, not speculation as to
its cause.

The Hebrew word for suffering is *yissurim,* which shares a
linguistic root with the word *mussar,* which means "to instruct."
Suffering contains lessons, but it is up to us to probe to discover
what our suffering can teach us.

The starting point is to be present and accepting of the fact that we are suffering, without running away in fear or anesthetizing ourselves or seeking comforts that we hope will mask the anguish. Our model here is the bitter herb (*maror*) that figures in the Passover seder meal. The horseradish or other sharp food we eat as *maror* reminds us of the embittered lives we led when we were slaves in Egypt. Bolting down the bitter herb does not fulfill the commandment to eat *maror,* because that doesn't give us the experience that contains the lesson; one must actually taste the bitterness. Similarly, we won't be able to grasp the lesson contained in our own suffering without first absorbing the bitterness that is its herald.[1]

In late 2011, Rabbi Nosson Tzvi Finkel passed away. He had been the rosh yeshiva of the Mir Yeshiva in Jerusalem, the largest yeshiva in the world, with over six thousand students. He was the grandson of his namesake, Rabbi Nosson Tzvi Finkel, who founded the Slobodka Yeshiva in Lithuania, which had such a profound impact on the contemporary Jewish world, and which had Mussar at its core.

The first thing anyone noticed about the Mir rosh yeshiva during the last twenty-eight years of his life was the effects of the Parkinson's disease that ravaged his body. At good times his body would merely shake; at harder times, he would thrash about spasmodically. When he would give a talk from a raised platform in the study hall, he would shake violently, with one arm tightly grasping the other so it wouldn't flail about on its own. Despite the pain and discomfort that was with him constantly, he mustered deep concentration as he delivered complicated and carefully nuanced thoughts on esoteric topics.

Most people with later-stage Parkinson's end up bedridden. In contrast, Rav Nosson Tzvi not only prayed regularly in the yeshiva and learned for many hours within its walls, he also built the biggest Torah community in the world during the time he was sick, taking massive financial responsibility for the yeshiva's growth onto his weary shoulders and still finding the time to impart warmth and love to his students. Until not long before his death, there was literally not a single decision made in the yeshiva, from the most important to the seemingly trivial, that did not pass through Rav Nosson Tzvi.

To help us learn the lesson of this quality that was so manifest in the life of Rav Nosson Tzvi Finkel, we have to make a distinction between suffering and pain, which are not the same thing. Pain is a direct reaction to an invasive stimulus and reflects simple cause and effect. Suffering, on the other hand, arises from interpretation and expectation. For example, pricking your finger with a needle and getting a health-inducing injection might score identically on a pain scale. But the suffering attached to the two may differ widely. Suffering invokes our sense of self, ego, entitlement, relationship to God, and everything else that goes into creating our relationship to the world in all its dimensions. "Ouch!" reflects pain. "Why me?" is about suffering.

We are wise to avoid unnecessary pain, if possible. But to avoid or deny or repress our suffering can stunt our growth. The question "Why me?" for example, may well not be answerable. My mother could never understand why she, who did not smoke and who exercised regularly, had a heart attack at a relatively young age, while her sisters, who both smoked and never exercised, did not. Accepting the disturbing and dislocating experience that the question points to involves contemplating and perhaps revising your notions of who you are, how much control you have over your life, how you relate to God's Will, and—most important of all—how you live.

In the face of incomprehensible tragedy, our minds are confounded and our hearts want to cry out. Shouldn't this world be a place of goodness and truth? Instead, we see evil, loss, selfishness, insensitivity, and random hurt. When we accept that such givens are part of the design of the world—even if we cannot make sense of them and even as we do our best to alleviate them, as we should—we have connected ourselves to truth and reality. So it is. We see this attitude demonstrated by Aharon after his two sons die as a result of bringing a forbidden fire offering. In his profound acceptance of what occurred, Aharon's response was to remain silent.[2]

Not only dramatic and life-and-death circumstances but even small and mundane disappointments can cause us to suffer. Our sages said, "To what extent does suffering go? Even if one reaches into a pocket to remove three coins and comes up with only two."[3] That's all it takes for the sun to disappear from our lives. Whether the cause is large or small, suffering is suffering; our challenge is to accept that we are suffering as the basis for going forward with our lives.

Acceptance is the source of the dedication and persistence that made Rabbi Nosson Tzvi Finkel unstoppable until the disease ran its course. He was born in America—where he was known as Nat—grew up on baseball, but then transcended that life to become a great leader, inspiring tens of thousands of students. His incredible self-sacrificing devotion is a model that can inspire us to strive to endure our own suffering and not let it cause us to deviate from our path of spiritual growth.

Acknowledging the truth of the world *as it is* forms a solid foundation for the transformation that is the acquisition of Torah.

PRACTICE

Identify one source of suffering in your life at this time. It may help to recall the distinction between pain and suffering—you are looking for some dark and uncomfortable feeling that reflects an aspect of your life that is other than you wish it were. It could be a physical or psychological or social or financial or other form of affliction about which you might feel "If only I didn't have that burden, then I'd focus more on my priorities and my spiritual life."

Can you accept that disturbing and dislocating feeling of disjuncture between reality and wish? In doing so, can you enter into peace with your suffering, as opposed to pushing it away or burying it or reacting to it? This is not a call to fatalism, as you may yet take vigorous action, but to peel back to the core of your feelings and to accept that this is your reality, your starting point in the now. Reach your arms around your sadness and loss. Expand your inner being so that you can let your feelings sit undisturbed in your chest.

Pay attention to what happens within you when you really do accept your suffering as your lot.

מכיר את מקומו

[25]

Knowing One's Place

Makir et Mekomo

How awesome is this place. It is no place other than the house
of God, and this is the gate of heaven.

—GENESIS 28:17

"PLACE" has great significance in Jewish thinking. Your existence in this world is defined by the space you occupy, and
only so long as you occupy that space are you part of this world.

Where you are defines your relationship to the world around
you: When a person makes a blessing over food, that blessing is
effective only as long as he or she remains in the place where the
blessing was said. A significant change of place requires that the
blessing be recited over again.

Another example is the distinction between private and
public domains. Many of the restrictions that apply on Shabbat
have to do with the boundaries of the place that you inhabit and
what you do that causes objects to move from one place to another.

The most mysterious but illustrative example of the importance of place is that one of the names of God is HaMakom—

which literally means "the Place."[1] God does not have a place; rather, God *is* the Place of the universe.

We learn from these and many other examples that the key thing about a place is that it has dimensionality that permits it to hold and restrict something else. We are not talking here about not stepping out of line in the social order, but of being present to the reality of the particular space or spaces that you occupy, in many dimensions of reality.

This notion shows up in our personal lives in regard to the inner trait of humility, which I have defined as "occupying your rightful place." You are meant to play a unique role in life, and that role has dimensionality that is yours to occupy. A key aspect of wisdom is to know who you are and where you fit into greater schemes. Occupying too much space (call that arrogance) and occupying too little of the dimension that is yours (call that self-deprecation) are equally major barriers to growing into wholeness.

According to the Maharal, knowing your place refers to self-knowledge.[2] You must have an honest assessment of yourself in order to acquire Torah. Otherwise, the basis for learning and transformation will be false and the results skewed. At the same time, knowing where you are at this moment creates the possibility of experiencing the awesome profundity that is accessible everywhere and always, if you open to it. In the wilderness and with only a stone for a pillow, Jacob proclaimed, "How awesome is this place." As is this place.

To acquire Torah, you must know the place that is yours in this moment and occupy it fully. That is not a one-time process, however, because our relationship to the world around us is constantly in motion. That shifting relationship only comes to an end when we are laid to rest in our final place.

We all know that we will ultimately occupy an unchanging

and final place, but that knowledge tends to be intellectual. It is very hard to grasp that our time on earth is limited, and that we have no idea when the moment of its ending will come. We tend to live as if death isn't real and won't touch us. Yet this is delusion. Our teachers encourage us to recall the reality of death not to be morbid or depressing but to cause us to wake up to the preciousness that radiates within every moment of life. You have the gift of being here, now, in this place. Occupy it fully. Don't waste this gift! Live a responsible life of purpose before it is too late!

The story is told about two men who came to Rabbi Chaim of Volozhin to resolve a dispute over ownership of a piece of land. After both men had explained their claim, Rabbi Chaim bent over and put his ear to the ground. The men had no idea what he was doing, and so he explained. Both men had laid claim to the land, and now he wanted to hear what the land had to say. He reported that the land said both men were making a big mistake: It was not they who owned the land, but rather they would eventually belong to it. His point was to challenge them: Why are you getting so caught up in the mundane and material and forgetting the profound and the spiritual?

The Alter of Kelm employed a visualization to make this point. He told of a town where the people had been so good that they merited an unusual boon: Their dead would come back to life, but only for half an hour. At the appointed time, the cemeteries emptied, and shades invaded the town. What did the dead do in their short time back among the living? They valued what the living took for granted and neglected, and each hastened to do studies and good deeds they had overlooked when they were alive.

Holding in mind the reality of death puts life in its proper perspective. Life is precious, but in the midst of it, we can forget what an exquisite—and temporary—gift has been given to us.

This is one of the explanations for why we smash a glass at a Jewish wedding. By shattering the vessel, we remind ourselves that all that is created and formed will eventually break. We temper our joy with a reminder of the fragility of life and our own ultimate mortality.[3] The same link is made in the traditional greeting that is recited to mourners, which refers to God by the name HaMakom—the Place—in wishing comfort to the bereaved.

Awareness of death can cause us to realize the spiritual potential and irreplaceable opportunity that inhabit every moment. The same Alter of Kelm explained a confounding teaching of the Talmud in just that way. Rav Hamnuna Zuti was asked to sing a song at a wedding feast, and so he launched into that entertaining ditty "Woe! We are dying! Woe! We are dying!"[4]

Why mention death at a wedding? The Alter's answer is that this reminder of mortality was meant as a challenge to the new couple to enhance their true *simcha* (joy) while they had the chance. As should we. Today. Right now! Here, in this place.

PRACTICE

Pirkei Avot 3:1 reads as follows:

> Akavya ben Mehalalel said: "Reflect upon three things and you will not come to the hands of sin. Know from where you have come, to where you are heading, and before Whom you will give justification and accounting. From where have you come—from a putrid drop; to where are you heading—to a place of dust, worms and maggots; and before Whom will you give justification and accounting—before the King Who reigns over kings, the Holy One, may He be blessed."

The text is saying directly that doing these visualizations, which are a core Mussar practice, will keep us from sin.

Our text focuses on "knowing your place" in a certain ultimate sense: the grave. Can you visualize your final resting place where your body will be placed in the earth? This is not easy to do, as we are generally averse to recognizing the truth of our mortality (except intellectually). But it is possible, and valuable, to do.

Imagine a plot of land, grass, a headstone, words written on that stone, including your name. Stay with that imagery for a few moments, exploring the visual details of your own grave. Have a good visit. Don't run away too soon.

Remembering death can give us a perspective that will help us with the decisions we face today. This visualization, while perhaps a bit uncomfortable, is a sure way to prevent mistaken decisions based on transient criteria (which, incidentally, may just be a good working definition of *sin*).

שמח בחלקו

[26]

Happiness with Your Portion

Samayach be'Chelko

Ben Zoma said: "Who is rich? Those who are happy with their portion."

—PIRKEI AVOT 4:1

THE METHOD of acquiring Torah discussed in this chapter says nothing about being happy with the good you have received but rather refers to being glad for *whatever* you have received. I find it so easy to feel blessed when life goes my way, but what about when what happens is exactly the opposite of what I hope for? What if I get a terminal diagnosis or my dream collapses, or I face even trauma or catastrophe? Am I supposed to be happy with that portion, too?

Indeed, we are taught, "A person is obliged to bless God for evil as well as good."[1] This is a challenging notion, until we understand its basis. The core message here is that we are not the best judges about what we receive. Can any of us say with certainty that we know what is best or even good for us in the long run? How many times in your own life has the thing that looked to be such a blessing turned out to be a curse, while the affliction carried within it seeds of a great and beautiful flowering? It is well known that many people who win huge lottery prizes discover very quickly that the envy, greed, animosity, and dislocation set in motion by their prize make them wish they had just torn up the ticket.

If you are happy with your portion, you can live sanely within your means and according to your true and deepest priorities. The Torah is explicit in saying that we are here on earth for one purpose only: to be holy. It does not carry us in that direction to be endlessly pursuing more, or newer, or bigger things or experiences, or, alternatively, to be spending our time and energy spinning in the eddies of regret. Being happy with your portion helps to keep material cravings in check. It also helps us take note of and appreciate the blessings that are already in our lives rather than obsessing about what we lack.

We have to notice that the teaching does not say that we should be content with what we have but rather *happy* with our portion. You may be working toward something else that is a reasonable goal, but that should not preclude celebrating the gifts you have in hand right now, because, from a certain perspective, this present moment and its circumstances are *perfect,* and that is surely a cause for joy.

I can remember the very old car I drove when I was a graduate student. It was an AMC Hornet that had served me well but was reaching the end of the road. I made a deal to trade it in for a new Honda, but delivery of the new car would take a month, during which time I continued to drive my Hornet. In that last month, the Hornet's transmission started to fail. One by one, I lost my gears until the only one that worked was reverse. I parked the car in my driveway until the call came to pick up my new car. When it did, I somehow had to get that old and limping Hornet to the dealership.

If I were in that situation today, I'd call a tow truck. Back then, I lived on a shoestring and thought more creatively. I figured out that if I made the trip early in the morning and stuck to the alleyways, I could back up all the way from home to the car showroom. And that's what I did, reversing through the city lanes and then darting backward across main streets until I drove onto the dealer's lot, rear end first.

What should I have felt? Pained regret that I was missing my three forward gears? Or great happiness that I still had reverse to get me to my destination?

This method of acquiring Torah is not concerned with things themselves. It isn't saying that having an old car is preferable to having a new one, or that you should necessarily do without a car entirely. Rather, it is teaching us about the quality of heart we should bring to our material life, and it is specifying that quality as happiness. We tend to get caught up in craving the things we feel we lack or being attached to what is already ours or regretting what we have lost. These feelings can take over our lives and distract us from more important, though less tangible, goals. The result can be misery in the place where we could have joy. We should each live within our means, be happy with the gifts we have, and not be covetous or envious of the possessions enjoyed by others.

Rav Dessler once taught a student a lesson about this very thing.

The student asked Rav Dessler for permission to attend a local flea market. Rav Dessler not only gave permission, he said he would like to accompany the young man to the market.

The two set out together and began to peruse the stalls. After some time, the student set eyes on a beautiful lamp. He bargained with the vendor until the seller agreed to a price. At that point Rav Dessler told the boy that he would really like to have that lamp for himself and asked if he could purchase it. Though disappointed, because he really wanted it, the student replied, "Of course, *rebbe*[2] can purchase the lamp for himself."

A little later the student spotted an elaborate silver goblet that he wanted to purchase. Again, no sooner had he finalized the deal than Rav Dessler told him that he wanted the goblet for himself, and again the boy agreed that he could have it. This went on a few more times until in total frustration the boy suggested that maybe it was time to return to the yeshiva.

When they were back, Rav Dessler called to speak to the boy. He brought out all of his purchases and handed them to the boy. "I didn't really want these things for myself. It's just that I saw how excited you got about them. I felt you needed to be cooled down. Now that you are settled, you can have them."

Desire, covetousness, and envy can knock us off our inner center, yet the Talmud teaches us that it is futile to feel dissatisfaction with what has been allotted to us as compared to others.[3] "No person can touch what was appointed for his fellow, even a hair's breadth," it says. That means there is a rightness to what you have in your possession. If God wants you to have more, you will, and if not, you won't. We certainly have an obligation to make efforts on our own behalf, but we should not fall prey to believing that our success or failure is determined by those efforts. Work hard, and then be happy with the portion you get allocated.

Advice to be happy with your portion could be mistaken for direction to be passive and unambitious, but that's not correct. Let's assume you are here to be active and productive, and let's also assume you actually accomplish something that you set out to do. Without this trait of being happy with your portion, you wouldn't get one minute of pleasure and satisfaction from your accomplishment. You wouldn't lift a glass to celebrate, you wouldn't feel the calm and contented feeling of completion. In fact, the drive to bigger, higher, better, more will have you back in the trenches without a break, as if you hadn't really accomplished anything at all. What kind of living is that?

PRACTICE

List five things you have that you feel are worthy of gladness. Here, to make it easier, is a start:

1. _____

2. _____

3. _____

4. _____

5. _____

Take a moment to appreciate and celebrate these things that have been given to you as your portion.

עושה סייג לדבריו

[27]

Making a Fence around Your Activities

Oseh Siyag Lidvarav

With cunning make your battle.

—PROVERBS 24:6

IT GOES RIGHT to the heart of the Jewish approach to life and growth to recognize that there are certain cliffs each of us is liable to fall over. In fact, I once heard my Mussar teacher, Rabbi Perr, say, "Sometimes you have to go right up to the edge of the cliff. And then fall over." Are we incapable of learning any other way? In place of lessons learned by landing on our heads, we can build fences to keep us away from the dangerous precipice in the first place. That idea may seem like common sense, which it is, but it is also of biblical origin.[1]

Generally speaking, the sages made decrees that forbade certain things that were actually permissible in order to keep us from getting close to the danger that lay just beyond them. Those fences fall into three categories:

1. Actions that outwardly resemble a transgression. In a Jewish context, an example would be eating chicken with milk, which is prohibited as an extension of the Torah commandment not to mix red meat and milk.
2. Actions that easily lead to a transgression due to the habits of everyday life. In Jewish law, it is forbidden to discuss business on Shabbat because words of business could easily lead to the writing of an agreement or making a payment, which are actually prohibited labors.
3. An act that leads to sin, even though it itself is permissible. Climbing a tree on Shabbat is not directly prohibited, but it could lead to breaking a branch, which is forbidden, and so climbing the tree gets outlawed.

In each of these cases, you can see that a protective barrier gets established some distance from the worrisome cliff itself, to prevent us from even getting close to going over the edge. The fence creates a margin of safety against the actual transgression that is of concern.

Rabbeinu Yonah explains that a person who truly fears doing wrong will willingly make protective fences around prohibited activities.[2] An analogy would be having dangerous medications in the house. Even though the drug containers may come equipped with "childproof" caps, the wise person will establish a fence by hiding them out of children's sight or reach.

Ramban adds a dimension to this teaching by showing us that fences can have a helpful role even in regard to activities that are permitted to us. We'd all understand the value of a fence to keep us from sexual misconduct, but Ramban says we also need fences to keep us from overindulging in sensuality in a sanctified relationship. The same is true of food and drink.

Fences can help keep us away from forbidden foods (be that un-kosher or unhealthy), but they can also help us stay far from the excesses of gluttony or drunkenness even with food or drink that is pristinely kosher or healthy. He makes these comments in his interpretation of the verse "*kedoshim tihiyu*"—you shall be holy—in which he teaches the crucial role fences can play in helping us develop self-restraint.

The way Rabbi Yerucham Levovitz explains this teaching is that when we are operating in an area where physical pleasure or sensation is involved, we must have strong intelligence ruling over us, because when the order is reversed and pleasure takes the lead, danger lurks.[3] Our intelligence isn't so strong when the passions are aroused, so we need fences to help keep us in the territory where our intelligence can fulfill its overseeing task.

The Hebrew word *devar* that is part of this current method of acquiring Torah can mean either "thing" or "word," so some interpret this particular method as making a fence around your words, and others call on us to make a fence around our activities. There is a story in the Talmud that brings the two meanings together:[4]

Captive women were brought for safe keeping to the house of the great and pious Rav Amram, who put them in the attic and then removed the heavy ladder to assure that there was no way to ascend. As one of the women passed by the opening between the attic and the house, a light illuminated her. Rav Amram caught sight of the woman and grabbed hold of the ladder, which ordinarily took ten men to lift, put it in place, and started to climb. Halfway up, he set his feet firmly on the rung and cried out loudly, "A fire at Rav Amram's house! A fire at Rav Amram's house!" People came running with buckets to extinguish the blaze, but they couldn't find any flames to douse.

Rav Amram taught that it was better that he embarrass himself than commit a sin.

Rav Amram put up fences to keep himself away from transgression with the captive women.[5] You might think that his fences failed, but they didn't. The fence, or, in this case, the ladder, couldn't keep him from experiencing desire; but, because he had established a distance from and an obstacle to acting on that desire, he had time between the flaming of the match and the igniting of the fuse in which to take a further preventive step. And, in that case, his action was words. His words built a fence that prevented him from doing what the ladder did not.

The Mussar teachers tell us that a *tzaddik* (a righteous person) is someone who runs far away from the *yetzer ha'ra*. That person doesn't just flee, however, because where can you go that the *yetzer ha'ra* doesn't follow, even if your name is Rav Amram HaChassid (the Pious)? The escape only makes it possible to take further action—to erect a trail of barricades and obstacles behind you, including praying, learning, studying, and practicing Mussar.

Each of us has cliffs to which we are drawn. For some it is sexual desire, for others wealth or possessions, for others still, honor, for many, calories. It could be wasting time or overindulging in permitted things. Our rabbis taught: Build fences. But be careful not to put the fence right at the edge of the cliff. Set it back a bit, so if it does happen that you jump over it, you still have hope of taking further steps to save yourself from a nasty fall.

PRACTICE

Identify one cliff that you are attracted to. You can do that by first thinking of some things that really are no temptation for you at all. You might find no attraction to gambling at a casino, for example, or you may not even like chocolate. But for someone else, those are the very cliffs that draw them siren-like and where real danger of transgression and harm lurks. What draws you toward a fall?

Once you have identified that cliff, devise a fence that you can erect that is a distance back from the precipice. For example, if your cliff involves eating cookies, it won't be enough just to get the cookies out of the cupboard and into the freezer. Frozen cookies are perfectly edible to me, and the microwave is always near at hand. The fence might be the front door of your house, where no cookie shall enter.

To extend to the example of gambling, it may not be enough to put your bank and credit cards in a drawer or even a safety deposit box. You might need to cut them up.

Like that, identify your own proclivity to transgress and establish a fence to keep you safely away from the sheer drop.

Is there anything that keeps you from building that fence right now?

[28]

Not Claiming Credit for Oneself

Eino Machazik le'Atzmo

Rabban Yochanan ben Zakkai received [the oral tradition] from Hillel and Shammai. He used to say, "If you have learned much Torah, do not claim credit for yourself, because you were created for that purpose."

—PIRKEI AVOT 2:8

WE LIVE IN a world in which people eagerly take credit for anything they can put their name to, even dubious achievements. Politicians give their names to laws, scientists embed their names in the labels they give to their discoveries, philanthropists plaster their names across buildings, astrophysicists call stars after themselves, actresses give names to perfumes, and many an activist heads a foundation bearing his or her own name.

How counter to this culture is one who takes no credit, even for great accomplishments. When Rabbi Yerucham Levovitz considered the question of who is destined for the World-to-Come,[1] he quoted the Talmud, which includes among this group the "constant student of Torah who takes no credit for himself."[2] Rav Yerucham explained that one who wants to earn that ultimate reward should look on himself or herself as obligated to serve the Creator in all the ways for which he or she has been endowed. A person should not seek or expect recognition for doing no more than what is incumbent upon him or her to do. Where does personal credit come into this picture?

This practice for acquiring Torah demands humility, and in the face of that, it might seem the height of arrogance for Rabbi Yisrael Salanter to have said, as he is quoted, "I know that I have the mental capacity of a thousand men." The accusation of inflated ego would be warranted if that's where he stopped, but in fact he went on: "Because of that, my obligation is also that of a thousand men." And that's where this method stretches beyond humility. The point here is that your talents create an obligation: You must put them to good use. At the same time, you need to recognize that you are due no credit for the talents themselves, which you only received as the unique gifts of your human life. At root, they are surely not your creation.

This approach applies in whatever ways a person is accomplished. The more wealth one has, the more that creates an obligation to help those in need. A wise person has responsibility to bring other people to understanding. A beautiful person can use his or her beauty to draw others to good causes. The fact that you may have greater abilities than someone else does not mean that you are better and that you can claim credit for your endowment, but only that you bear responsibilities because you have received gifts, and that obligates you.

I have felt the tension in my own life between an innate compulsion to brag about accomplishments and the spiritual precept that urges me to recognize that nothing I have done is independent of gifts I have received, for which I cannot possibly claim credit. Being a Rhodes scholar is something that people hold in high regard because it implies excellence in a number of fields. In my case, I was active in university sports (hockey and football), ran for student government, got straight A's in my courses, and so on. The ego is hungry to say, "Hey, look at me. I did all that. Aren't I great?" In point of fact, however, could I have played sports without the healthy, capable body that I was blessed to have and the good nutrition my parents worked hard to provide? Nutrition played a role in my academic accomplishments, as well, as did the mind that is my natural endowment. Even if you argue that I had to work hard to make the most of those gifts, I'll respond to ask if I can take credit for my motivation or ambition or even the pleasure I got from being accomplished in various areas? It begins to seem foolish to claim any kind of personal credit for accomplishments.

When it comes to spiritual accomplishments, it seems obvious that bragging would be a contradiction, but that doesn't mean it isn't a temptation and that people don't do it. We do! Which is why it is necessary and useful for us to learn about this practice, so we can be cautioned to avoid the pitfall. Rabbi Moshe Chaim Luzzatto, also known as Ramchal, writes that even one who has attained great wisdom should consider that accomplishment as the result of having received the gift of mental ability, no different from a bird that soars on its wings or a powerful bull that pulls the plow.[3] The realization that my abilities were given to me by my Creator spawns humility; and humility should cause me to acknowledge that my personal accomplishments do not come from *"kochi v'otzem yadi"*—my power and the might of my hand[4]—but rather from the gifts that have been bestowed on me.

The Talmud in one place mentions a student who cites a teaching by saying, "We said such-and-such there," and does not attribute the teaching to his teacher.[5] The Talmud brings forward this behavior as an example of an *apikorus* (generally a term applied to heretics). And the penalty? No share in the World-to-Come!

A person who takes credit for their accomplishments is like a thief. Whatever we achieve, we do not do it alone, and we must not steal the credit due to someone else. I'm writing, but I did not create the computer or the software I'm writing on or the electricity that powers my equipment. I did not create the language I speak. Present-day work stands on the shoulders of the giants of previous generations. What of the gifts and sacrifices of our parents? And our teachers? Ultimately, anything we do is possible only because we receive help from God. What kind of rational person could begin to take personal credit for his or her accomplishments?

Indeed, a humble person can be defined as someone who does not take credit for what he or she has done because the humble person is well aware of being the recipient of gifts from other people and God. If anything, such a person would consider how much more he or she ought to have accomplished with those gifts.

There is one exception to this categorical rejection of taking credit, and that concerns ethical choices. We can take credit for our ethical choices. If when faced with a dilemma or a temptation, I make a choice for the good, the credit is mine. Were that not the case, no one could hold me accountable and responsible for my transgressive ethical choices, either. Since we are responsible for the bad we choose, we must also be responsible for good choices, for which credit is due.

PRACTICE

Think of something good that you accomplished recently and then reflect on the factors that made that accomplishment possible. Did intelligence play a role? Strength? Perseverance? Sensitivity? Awareness? Or?

Now trace the source of every one of these capacities back far enough to see that your strengths are all the result of gifts you have received. In place of taking credit for the outcome, it makes much more sense that you will be grateful for receiving the gifts that made the accomplishment possible.

Not taking credit is made much more real by giving credit. Select one or two people whom you just listed and call or write to them to express your gratitude for the gifts they gave you that made possible your achievement.

אהוב

[29]

Being Beloved

Ahuv

> Three things make a person beloved by others: an open hand, a
> set table and a happy frame of mind.
>
> —AVOT D'RABBI NATAN 31

THE NEED to be loved is deeply embedded in the human
psyche, and being loved is a fulfilling experience in itself.
Not only that, when people love you, they want to help you.
They'll give you good advice and protect you from harm. A
beloved person ranks high on invitation lists and has advantages
in business. All areas of life benefit.

That fact leads to an important question: What makes a person lovable? More to the point, what makes *you* lovable? But
before we can answer that question, we have to ask another:
What is love?

There are so many definitions of love, from psychology to
song, and none of them seems to satisfy because we can't quite
put our finger on what love is. The Mussar view is helpful because it takes a very different approach, not even trying to define

love but rather focusing on awakening in us what generates the feelings, commitments, and bonds we call love.

The starting point for the Mussar teachers is the recognition that our primary inner nature is that of a soul. There are levels, or dimensions, to the soul, but only one concerns us in regard to love, and that is the *nefesh*-soul, which is the aspect of the inner life that is made up of all the emotions, character traits, and values that are specific to an individual. What we call love blossoms when two human beings draw so close to one another that their *nefesh*-souls merge.

This phenomenon is explained well in the sixteenth-century kabbalistic Mussar text called *Reishit Chochmah*, written by Rabbi Eliyahu de Vidas (1518–92). He writes that what we call "love" is in actuality the coming together of two separate souls to create a larger unit:

> Even though your body's material substance separates you from your friend, the *nefesh*-soul of both of you is a spiritual entity and the tendency of the spirit is to make you cleave to your friend with unbroken unity. When your *nefesh*-soul becomes aroused to love a friend, your friend's *nefesh*-soul will be equally aroused to love you in return until both of your souls are bound to form one single entity.[1]

As proof, he points to the biblical verses that describe the love between David and Jonathan:

> And it came to pass that the *nefesh*-soul of Jonathan was knit with the *nefesh*-soul of David, and Jonathan loved him as his own *nefesh*-soul. Then Jonathan made a

covenant with David, because he loved him as his own *nefesh*-soul.[2]

It is not that these two friends loved each other because their souls knit together, nor did their souls cleave to one another because of their love; rather, *love* is a term we use to name the spiritual reality of two souls connecting and cleaving into one unit, knitting together. Love is the emotional experience of *achdut ha'oheiv ve-ha'ahuv*—the unity of the lover and the beloved. In over two hundred places in the Torah, the word *ahavah* appears to describe the unity of man and woman, of master and servant, of family, of the neighbor and the stranger, and, of course, of seeker and God.

The experience of "falling in love" in Jewish thought is rooted in destiny. When two souls that are meant for one another meet, the deep recognition is instantaneous and the bond immediate. Rav Yehuda is quoted in the Talmud as saying in the name of (a different) Rav: "Forty days before the creation of a child, a heavenly voice issues forth and proclaims, 'The daughter of this one is for that one.'"[3] The divinely ordained spouse is a true soul mate, called *basherte* (female) or *basherter* (male) in Yiddish.

Destined love can give rise to an instantaneous recognition, the proverbial eyes meeting across the room. Or it can emerge through long exposure and the hard work that can go into building a relationship. In cultures where marriages are arranged, there is an expectation that love will grow in time, nurtured by commitment and shared experience.

Now that we know that it is the merger of souls that generates love, what can we do to become beloved? King Solomon provides an answer by saying, "As water reflects a face, so does a person's heart."[4] This means that whatever you project from your heart is what you can expect to receive in return. If you take no interest in others, they will take no interest in you. If, on the other hand, you are warm and caring, you can also expect to attract warmth to yourself.

I have seen this principle at work. I give students who are working to develop the quality of honor (*kavod*) the assignment of imitating the behavior of the Talmudic sage Rabbi Yochanan ben Zakkai. It is reported that Rav Yochanan was quick to greet every person he met before the other person could greet him.[5] When students start doing this greeting practice, they find that their friendly greetings are almost always returned in kind, their smiles are repaid in smiles. Suddenly, the usually cold and unfriendly world melts into a place of warmth and friendliness. All because they projected something different from their hearts.

What we see here reflects Rabbi Eliyahu Dessler's insightful teaching on love.[6] He notices the connection between love and generosity, and he asks which comes first. Do we give to the person we love, or do we love the person we give to? He concludes that love follows giving. When you give to someone, be it a smile, a hand, some time, money, goods (according to their need), that sets the stage for love to grow. The key to being beloved is therefore to be generous, to have an open hand. The text quoted at the head of this chapter mentions "a set table," which is also a form of generosity.

Too often, we seek love from a place of need and want. We may not have realized that we become beloved by giving to others and feeding them (literally and metaphorically).

But how does being beloved help us to work the transformation that is called acquiring Torah? The Maharal suggests an interesting answer to this question: Only one who makes himself or herself part of the community merits the Torah's wisdom, because Torah was given and continues to be given to the whole community, not to an individual. In a very famous comment,

Rashi notes that when the people encamped at Mount Sinai in order to receive the Torah, the community was so cohesive it was "like one person with one heart."[7] Only in the context of love like that—where hearts are united—can one acquire Torah, with all that means.

PRACTICE

The present focus tells us that everything flows out of being loved. We have learned that the best way to become beloved is to give your love to other people.

Your assignment is to identify one or two people to whom you can proactively seek to connect. Have a conversation or set up a visit and when you are with that other person, really be there for their sake, not your own gratification. Try to understand and appreciate them without harsh judgment, to give to them what *they* need and want, both physically and spiritually.

That's how you give love. That's how you become beloved. Rabbi Hanina ben Dosa (first century C.E.) used to say, "One who is pleasing to his fellow human, is pleasing to God. But one who is not pleasing to his fellow human, is not pleasing to God."[8]

Pay close attention to the response your efforts bring and see what you learn.

אוהב את המקום

[30]

Loving God

Ohev et ha'Makom

You shall love the Lord your God with all your heart and with
all your soul and with all your might.

—DEUTERONOMY 6:5

ANYONE WITH even a passing familiarity with Judaism
knows that, according to its teachings, we are supposed
to love God. Many verses in the Torah, some of which have
become part of the daily liturgy, tell us to love God. Famous
among these is "You shall love the Lord your God with all your
heart and with all your soul and with all your might." The obligation to love the Holy One is stated nine different times in the
five Books of Moses, which gives the commandment to love
God biblical roots. It is one of the first of the 613 *mitzvot* listed by
Maimonides (number 3, to be exact).

Yet we have to wonder, how can we possibly love what we
cannot see or touch or even conceive in our minds? Without a
clearly defined and tangible other, how can we love? That question could well stop us in our tracks, so we need a path forward.
We are fortunate that tradition provides one.

Rambam helps us out here by writing that a person can only love commensurate with the degree to which he or she *knows* the object of his or her love.[1] If one knows a little, one can love a little. And if one knows a lot, one can love a lot. Through study and life experience and contemplation, we can gain knowledge of God; and that will lead us toward loving God.

On this basis, we have to change our question. Instead of wondering how can we love God, we need to ask, How we can know God?

Rambam lived in the twelfth century. An even older Mussar source—*Duties of the Heart*, by Rabbi Bahya ibn Paquda, dating to the eleventh century—deals directly with the love of God. In chapter 10, "How Do We Come to the Love of God?," he describes the love of God as a human proclivity: "the demonstration of the soul's longing and inherent affinity for the Creator." Later in that chapter, he provides two methods by which we can come to know God: by "studying the books of the prophets and the words of the ancients" and by "reflecting upon the world as it exhibits some of God's wonders in creation."

These two methods, handed down about a thousand years ago, are still accessible and effective for us today.

With all the resources that exist in this present day, it's relatively easy to study Torah and Jewish history, and that study is as much about God as it is about the world, its people, and things that happened. And examining any aspect of the natural world ought to bring you to awesome awareness and appreciation. How can a hummingbird have such an iridescent throat? Who painted the butterfly's wings? How can the wonder that is a giraffe or a blue whale even be conceived? As Rambam himself writes, "When one contemplates God's great, wondrous actions and creatures and sees within them inestimable and boundless

divine wisdom, one immediately loves and gives praise and ex-
alts, and experiences great desire to know the great Name."[2]

Focusing on the second of these methods, in our time science has explored the frontiers of deep space as well as the atom,
two extremes of the created world. When we open our minds to
consider what actually exists in these dimensions of the physical
world, we come face to face with knowledge of the divinity that
stands behind it.

In 1995, the powerful Hubble Space Telescope was focused
on what appeared to be a nearly empty patch of sky. The area in
focus was tiny—about one 24-millionth of the whole sky,
equivalent to a 65-mm tennis ball as seen from a distance of
100 meters. The telescope absorbed the light emanating from
this corner of the sky for ten days, a long period for a telescope
that did most of its readings in a matter of hours. When the results were analyzed, what showed up in that tiny patch of apparently dark sky were three thousand galaxies, large and small,
floating in the depths of space. Each contained hundreds of billions of stars. The light that the telescope was receiving was itself
emitted billions of years ago. *Ha'shamayim misaprim kavod El*—
the very heavens declare God's majesty![3]

At the other end of the scale, for almost fifty years scientists
sought to prove the existence of the Higgs boson, a subatomic
particle that had been theorized but never observed. In pursuit
of this elusive tiny building block of creation, they built the
Large Hadron Collider, one of the world's most complex and
expensive experimental facilities, occupying a 27-km tunnel
underground near Geneva. So sophisticated a workshop was
needed because the theory called for the mysterious particle to
be extremely small and unstable, disappearing almost the instant
it appeared. In 2012, scientists accelerated a large number of

particles to extremely high energies and extremely close to the speed of light, then allowed them to smash together, with cameras taking forty million pictures per second. The Higgs boson was confirmed, and with that discovery came a new possibility of explaining all the mass in the universe. Everything that has mass gets it by interacting with the Higgs field, which occupies the entire universe. No wonder the Higgs boson has been nicknamed "the God particle."

When you open your mind to the vastness and infinite complexity of the universe we inhabit—through contemplating things like the mind-boggling examples I have given here but equally in the apparently ordinary things we see every day, from the flight of a bird to the pollinating lives of bees to the ability of your eyes to see these words and your brain to turn them into thoughts—you will come to know more of God. From that knowledge will flow love for the Creator.

It is easy to write about loving God and hard to know what that means and how to do it. The essence of love is seeking connection, and each of us is charged with responsibility to cultivate this love relationship, this connection with the Source of all. Since we are all different from one another, we each have to find our own ways to connect. Some will get there through the intellect, others through prayer, song, or meditation. When you undertake to try to connect with God, and you don't lose sight of that focus during the process, the very act of seeking is the most effective means to forge that connection.

PRACTICE

Our goal is loving God, and our route to that goal is by way of knowing God. Where will you look to find God today? Bahya ibn Paquda has given us two suggestions. You can do either or both:

1. Study Torah and in particular the prophets, where the hand and presence of God is so evident. The book of Daniel is good for this purpose. We're looking to find a way to know God through this study, and God makes an appearance early in this book of prophecy: "In the third year of the reign of Jehoiakim, king of Judah, came Nebuchadnezzar, king of Babylon, unto Jerusalem, and besieged it. And the Lord gave. . . ."

2. Look into nature to see the wonders of creation. Just focus on one flower, one fruit, one creature, and look at its color, shape, and the systems that sustain it individually and in its habitat. You don't need to know the science or to go far to conduct this contemplation. Just pick up and consider an apple, for example.

[31]

Loving God's Creatures

Ohev et ha'Briyot

You shall love your neighbor as yourself.

—LEVITICUS 19:18

WE'VE JUST focused on loving God, and now we turn our love in the direction of earthly beings. If we have difficulty understanding how to love God because we don't know God well enough, we could have just the opposite problem loving God's creatures—because we know them all too well.

That might be true of people, but love of God's creatures actually is a more inclusive category that does not start with humanity. Rav Kook writes, "The love of all beings precedes everything else. Afterwards comes the love of all humanity. After that comes the love of the people of Israel."[1]

And indeed, the love we are encouraged to pursue in the direction of God is directly connected to this current transformative method. The Maharal wrote, "Love of all creatures is also love of God, for whomever loves the One loves all the works that God has made. When one loves God, it is impossible not to love God's creatures. The opposite is also true. If one hates the creatures, it is impossible to love God Who created them."[2]

We live on a beautiful and diverse planet, and our own development to our spiritual potential depends on loving the creatures we live among. As Rabbi Samson Raphael Hirsch says so clearly, "And as for the human being . . . , his heart has been created so tender that it feels with the whole organic world . . . so that if nothing else, the very nature of his heart must teach him that he is required above everything else to feel himself the kin of all beings, and to recognize the claim of all beings to his love and beneficence."[3]

All these sources point to the love we need to cultivate for the squirrels and the robins, the pythons and the macaques. Too often, people view the natural world not in terms of tender-hearted love but from a utilitarian perspective, calculating the use and value that we can extract from its nonhuman inhabitants. That attitude has caused species to be hunted to extinction and others to be subjugated to oppressive living conditions, like the geese that are caged en masse and force fed to produce foie gras, or the production of veal, which typically involves removing calves from their mothers shortly after birth and raising them in special cages that restrict movement so the flesh will be extra tender to the taste.

The activist focus on animal welfare or species preservation is outward looking, concerned with the well-being of the animals, whereas the injunction to love other creatures that we encounter here also invokes an inward focus, concerned for the effect our treatment of other creatures has on our own hearts. When we treat animals as nothing more than a resource to be exploited, we not only do harm to those animals, we also cause the heart within us to become shriveled and hardened. It is to counteract that consequence that we are encouraged to practice loving other creatures. Only the tender heart is receptive to the transformative possibility that is called acquiring Torah.

From the exercise of loving the animals, we move on to the greater challenge of loving God's human creations. Many of us find this hard because all people are flawed, all have a *yetzer ha'ra,* all do things we don't like. Yet we are taught in the Torah to "Love your neighbor as yourself," and about this verse Rabbi Akiva says, "This is a great principle of the Torah."[4] It may not come easily to love humanity, and that is exactly what makes it such a great and effective spiritual practice for cultivating the loving heart we seek.

As with loving God, it helps to have a practical hint about how to do it. Rav Kook provides one. He writes, "All these types of love express themselves in activity: loving others to do good for them and to improve them."[5]

Love in the Jewish tradition is incomplete if it is only a sentiment. It requires deeds in order to be actualized, both in the world and in our own hearts. It is not enough to hold good thoughts for the bride and groom; we need to kick up our heels in dance at the wedding to gladden them. It is not enough to send out comforting vibrations to someone in mourning; we need to bake a kugel and then take it in hand to the house of mourning. If we truly love someone, we want the best for them. Sometimes that "best" is to feed them or give them clothes to wear, but it could be to help them grow spiritually or just to be their companion. Love feeds action and is fed by it.

Our role model for love-in-action is Aharon, the high priest (*kohen gadol*) whose task it was to unify all of Israel in the worship of God. The Mishnah teaches, "Be among the disciples of Aharon, loving peace and pursuing peace, loving people and bringing them closer to Torah."[6] For him, this was not just a matter of feelings in his heart; it demanded action, as we see from the double expression in the verse "*ohev shalom* [love peace] *v'rodef shalom* [and pursue peace]." Loving others in your heart is not enough; you must express your love in deed, as well.

The *midrash* fills in the picture of how Aharon made peace between quarreling parties.[7] When he walked the street and came upon a wicked person, he would give that person a friendly greeting. The result was that when this wicked person would be tempted to sin, he would say to himself, "How can I do this? When I next see Aharon and he gives me his warm greeting, I'll be so embarrassed!"

The same source tells us that when two parties were quarreling, Aharon would go over to one and say, "See how upset the other person is, so much that he has torn his clothing in grief." He would then go to the other fellow and say the same thing. Each would feel so bad about causing such pain that they would kiss and make up.[8] Aharon was motivated by such great love for people that he was even willing to bend truth for the sake of establishing peace between them.[9]

All too often, people are interested in grand ways to save the planet or to advance humanity, but their personal lives are not consistent with the values they preach. When it comes to loving God's creatures, our inside must be like our outside.[10] We must love them in our hearts in order to cultivate the loving heart we seek, but we must also express that love in active, tangible behavior. That way, both the world we live in and the world within become more whole (*shalem*), and we and the world can live in peace (*shalom*).

PRACTICE

Identify someone whom you love or feel that you have the capacity to love. Focus on that person and really feel your desire to be loving to them.

Then put your mind to work to think of something you can do to show your love for that person. Feed them? Show them caring? Encourage their spiritual practice? Offer them company? This part is up to you, according to your own assessment of what the person needs that you can provide.

Now do it!

אוהב את התוכחות

[32]

Loving Rebukes

Ohev et ha'Tochechot

Rebuke a wise person and he will love you.

—PROVERBS 9:18

THIS METHOD of transformation is stated in the plural—
"rebukes"—and not the singular. Some interpreters say
that we are meant to understand from this that there are times
one needs to receive rebuke, and there are other circumstances
in which one needs to deliver a message intended to help someone else straighten their way. But we are not just to receive or
deliver rebuke. We are to "love rebuke," something we can understand and apply in two ways.

It is not enough to be "open to feedback." We have to recognize how irreplaceably valuable rebuke is, so that we see each
bit of mirroring we receive as a treasured gift. We should love it
because it is so good for us.

And we are to offer our feedback to others only in a loving
manner. Love is the secret ingredient that makes it possible to
deliver criticism in a way that will allow it to be heard. Rebuke

WITH HEART IN MIND

can only be effective when one hates the sin but loves the sinner. Without love, it's not rebuke but affront.

As for the feedback we receive, we need it, and mostly we dislike getting it. We need it because we are all masters of self-deception, and so only feedback from others gives us a more accurate reading of the state of our *middot* as others experience them. And we hate getting it because we are not humble. When someone tells us about a shortcoming or a way in which we have missed the mark, the ego springs to the defense. That is no strategy for growth.

Note that this method doesn't require us to love the one who delivers the rebuke nor to love receiving that sort of feedback, but only to love the rebuke itself. It's so easy to focus on (and shoot) the messenger and to find fault because the feedback was delivered in this way or that. We are guided here to avoid those deflections. Pay careful attention only to the message and what it has to teach you about yourself. That's what is precious.

When I worked as a film producer, I often had to give writers feedback on their scripts. The typical writer would resist every question or suggestion, but one writer had a very different attitude. Whenever he was offered feedback, he would welcome it enthusiastically with the words, "Come on! Make me look good!" What this teaching is inviting us to say in response to rebuke is slightly different: "Come on! Make me *be* good!"

Rabbeinu Yonah of Gerona said basically the same thing in the thirteenth century:[1]

Listen well, surrender yourself, and return in repentance when you are admonished by sages and those who criticize you. Take each word of criticism to heart without exception. By doing that, you will go from darkness to great light in an instant. For if you listen and internalize

. . . , repent and take the words of those who criticize you to heart . . . your repentance will take effect, and you will become an entirely different person. So search hard for those who would offer you criticism and learn from whoever will teach you.

Not all feedback is accurate, of course. Someone who rebukes you may be deluded or even malicious. Even then, you should scour their words to see if there is anything in them that rings true for you that you could accept and work on.

In addition to loving the rebuke you receive, you need to be sensitive to how you deliver your own feedback. Yes, it is an obligation to offer input to correct the ways of others, as the Torah emphasizes by saying, "You shall surely rebuke."[2] But the completion of the verse is "and do not bear sin because of him." The sin in question could well come from being hurtful even as you try to be helpful.

The problem we face here is not new. In the Talmud, Rabbi Tarfon, who lived around the first century C.E., is quoted as saying, "In this generation there is no one capable of delivering rebuke." His contemporary, Rabbi Elazar ben Azariah, added, "In this generation there is no one capable of receiving rebuke." Rabbi Akiva then said, "In this generation there is no one who knows how rebuke ought to be worded."[3] It seems not much has changed in the past 1,500 years.

Despite this, we see a remarkable example of loving rebuke in a story Rav Wolbe retold from Rabbi Yechezkel Sarna (1890–1969),[4] who was present when Rav Wolbe's teacher, Rabbi Yerucham Levovitz, met with his own teacher, the Alter of Slobodka.[5] At the meeting, the Alter harshly criticized Rav Yerucham for the way he dealt with his students. Rav Yerucham listened quietly and did not respond. Rav Sarna was certain that

Rav Yerucham would not quickly return after such a welcome. To his surprise, Rav Yerucham came back the very next day. This time, the Alter criticized Rav Yerucham even more sharply. Now and then Rav Yerucham would seek to clarify the Alter's exact intention on a certain point, but he did not respond at all to the harsh critique. Now Rav Sarna was positive Rav Yerucham would not return—but he was again mistaken! Rav Yerucham returned the next day to speak with the Alter and again was harshly criticized. This went on for a full week!

Lest you think the Alter of Slobodka was abusing a young student, this took place when Rav Yerucham was already *mashgiach* (spiritual advisor) to hundreds of students in the Mir Yeshiva. His mastery was such that he could be the epitome of strength and leadership when guiding students, and at the same time he was able to submit to the rebuke of his teacher. He exemplified what Rabbi Yisrael Salanter once wrote to his own student Rav Itzele Petersburg,[6] that he must sometimes be a "hero among heroes" (*gever b'guvrin*), strong willed and able to stand up for what he believed, no matter what.[7] At other times, however, he must be like a youngster (*tza'ir yamim*) who listens and accepts the criticism of others.

The Torah's story of Moses being criticized by his father-in-law, Yitro, models both sides of this lesson.[8] "Why do you sit alone with all the people standing by you from morning to evening?" Yitro asks. "The thing that you do is not good. . . . Now heed my voice, I will advise you, and may God be with you." Yitro, a foreigner, rebuked the leader of the entire nation and did so with the wish that "God be with you," showing his love. And imagine the humility it took for Moses to listen to what his father-in-law had to say! The result of this rebuke properly given and willingly received was that "Moses heeded the voice of his father-in-law, and did everything that he had said."

If you are inclined to shy away from rebuke, pay attention to what Rabbi Yehuda HaNasi (135–217 C.E.) taught in the Talmud: "What is the straight path that a person should travel? He should love rebuke, for at times when there is rebuke in the world, pleasantness comes to the world, goodness and blessing come to the world."[9]

PRACTICE

At some point in these days it is likely that you will see or hear someone doing something that is out of line. You might feel the impulse to look the other way or just hold your peace, but in the spirit of this lesson, you should undertake to give them your rebuke (though *feedback* might be a more palatable word in our times).

Before you do that, however, check in within yourself to ensure that you are acting out of love, that your words will be spoken with love, and that you are far from anger and judgment. If these are conditions you can't meet, it isn't the right time for you to give that feedback. Work more on processing your feelings until you are ready to reach out to redirect your friend or colleague or family member with love.

And should it happen that someone gives *you* corrective feedback, receive it with love and appreciation and take it to heart.

אוהב את המישרים

[33]

Love of Uprightness

Ohev et ha'Meisharim

Tzedek, tzedek tirdof—righteousness you shall surely pursue.

—DEUTERONOMY 16:20

THERE IS SOME controversy over this item in the list from *Pirkei Avot*. Some have *ohev et ha'tzedakot* (love justice) in this place, while others, including Rashi, the Vilna Gaon, and *Midrash Shmuel,* have only *ohev et ha'meisharim* (love of uprightness).

The word *Ha'Meisharim,* "uprightness," comes from the root *yashar,* meaning "straight." This method for transforming ourselves directs us to love doing the right things, even things that go beyond what we are obligated to do. Loving righteousness requires a heartfelt commitment to fairness, justice, assisting the weak and oppressed, and a real willingness to extend ourselves for those causes.

Rabbi Yisrael Salanter's pursuit of righteousness was Mussar in action. It once came to his attention that a wealthy man had bribed the local authorities so that the son of a widow would be drafted into the army in place of his own son. Rabbi Salanter went to the local synagogue, and when the wealthy man rose to lead prayers, Rav Yisrael cried out, "It is forbidden for you to lead us in prayer, for you are a heretic. You don't believe in God or the Torah! You pray only because your father prayed. If you really believed that the Torah was the voice of God commanding you, how would you dare ignore Torah laws which forbid oppressing a widow and favoring prominent people in judgment?"

Rav Salanter's rebuke is based in Jewish principles of social justice. Certain forms of social action (like giving charity and caring for the poor and needy) are commanded, while others (like oppressing widows, orphans, and the strangers among us) are prohibited. The pursuit of righteousness in a Jewish way is not a feel-good kind of thing that would have us jump into action when our heart feels moved. It is our obligation to see that justice is done and others cared for, regardless of how we might be feeling at that moment.

The pursuit of social justice is essential to spiritual life. Rabbi Salanter put it well, saying that, "The spiritual is superior to the material. But the material needs of another are an obligation of my spiritual life." My own soul journey requires that I help others in practical ways. Yet our current method doesn't tell us to "observe" or "adhere to" or even "pursue" righteousness; rather, it says, "Love righteousness." To reap the maximum spiritual impact, our hearts need to be fully invested in our world-healing actions. This is a matter of commitment, not sentiment. Righteousness then becomes the moral foundation for our lives; and, ultimately, through deeds we do that help others, our hearts are straightened, and we and our world become infused with holiness.

These principles come into play in regard to giving charity. The Hebrew word for charity is *tzedakah,* derived from the root *tzedek,* which means "justice." Defining giving to the needy not as benevolent kindness but as a matter of justice establishes that supporting the poor is a social duty. Charity is then not a sign of magnanimity but rather an action that emerges from an understanding of what is *due* to the poor. *Tzedakah* is cast more as wisdom than good-heartedness because it is based on an understanding of the world, its ways, and the responsible place we and others have in it.

Feeling responsibility and acting on that sense of obligation is a transformative catalyst for the heart. Rabbi Chaim Shmulevitz (1902–79), rosh yeshiva of the Mir Yeshiva in Poland, Shanghai, and Jerusalem, writes that a person achieves greatness by accepting responsibilities. The "diligent person whose life is guided by effort and self-restraint is elevated to heights bordering on the divine."[1] The more responsibility for others that a person takes on, the greater he or she becomes. Shouldering responsibility for others can be a path to greatness, regardless of whether that responsibility is a matter of obligation or taken on voluntarily.

When we remind ourselves that the root notion at work here is straightness, it is easy to identify the many different ways we are vulnerable to being bent and twisted away from the straight path. The epitome of Jewish spiritual experience is to bask in the light of the *Shechina*, the divine presence, and the Talmud lists four types of people before whom the *Shechina* does not appear.[2] These are scoffers, flatterers, liars, and slanderers.[3] Each of these tendencies represents a departure from the straight way. Each uses words to try to twist a situation in the direction of self-interest.

Take flattery (*chanifa*). We tend to flatter people who have influence or power that we believe could help us achieve one of our goals. Our flattering words have no allegiance to truth or even-handedness, and so uttering them damages our inner sense of righteousness and honesty. When we flatter, we sacrifice the straightness of the means in order to achieve a desired end, and then we pay the big price of becoming shallow and fake. Phony people don't merit real spiritual experiences like having the *Shechina* rest on them.

The opposite of the scoffers, flatterers, liars, and slanderers is the person who holds to his or her principles despite the potential losses that such loyalty might cause. The term *mesirat nefesh* literally means "giving over the soul" and refers to someone who willingly makes a sacrifice for the sake of a higher principle. The sacrifice for the sake of a cause can be economic or go so far as to cost the person his or her very life. Nothing great has ever happened in this world except that someone put a higher purpose ahead of personal self-interest.

When the soul comes into the world, its circle of interest and engagement is very small. Much effort in child rearing goes into guiding the child to be less selfish, more inclusive of others in thought and action. As parents put their own needs for sleep, food, and pleasure second to the needs of their child, they are engaged in growing beyond self-interest. From a soul perspective, life is meant to be a journey of expanding the boundaries of the self to include family, friends, spouse, community, and more, depending on the nature and potential of that soul.

The more a person identifies with a personal "I," the smaller the world he or she inhabits, and the less motivation there is to be upright in dealing with others. The more expansive the sense of who is included in the definition of "I," the more obvious and natural it is to treat everyone within that expanded boundary with righteousness.

This is a teaching of Rabbi Shimon Shwab,[4] in his book *The Gates of Uprightness*:

The entire "I" of a coarse and lowly person is restricted only to his substance and body. Above him is someone who feels that his "I" is a synthesis of body and soul. And above him is someone who can include in his "I" all of his household and family. Someone who walks according to the way of the Torah, his "I" includes the whole Jewish people, since in truth every Jewish person is only like a limb of the body of the nation of Israel. And there are more levels.[5]

When approached in this way, uprightness and responsibility are not a matter of diminishing the individual ego or suppressing self-interest. Rather, we are being shown that we have the potential to expand the boundaries within which we live beyond the self. Expanding in this way is a step toward actualizing the soul's potential, or, as we might say, acquiring Torah.

PRACTICE

Be attentive and sensitive to how you use words. Are your words straight as arrows, or do they twist and turn to try to curry favor? Be especially sensitive to the motivation that leads you to give praise. Was the talk really that good? Was the meal that delicious? Was the gift that generous? Or can you detect a willingness to exaggerate and bend the truth to achieve a self-serving goal?

Be on the lookout for the urge to flatter, whether spread on thickly (as in Yiddish, where the act of flattery is referred as to *shmeeren*) or in subtle ways.

מתרחק מן הכבוד

[34]

Distancing from Honor

Mitrachek min ha'Kavod

Rabbi Elazar Ha'Kapar said, "Envy, desire and the pursuit of honor put a person out of the world."

—PIRKEI AVOT 4:21

AT THE AGE of eleven, Yaakov Yisrael Kanievsky (1899–1985) entered yeshiva to study under Rabbi Yosef Yozel Horowitz (1847–1919), the founder of the Novarodok school of Mussar. That young boy eventually became famous as the Steipler,[1] one of whose teachings concerned the dictator Herod, who taught his parrots to call out "*Melech! Melech!*" ("King! King!") every time he passed by. The Steipler reminds us that Herod had been born a slave and usurped power to become king. He needed to be reminded that he was no longer a slave, a pursuit of honor born out of insecurity.

This is the nature of the pursuit of honor (*kavod*). People seek honor in the hope of filling an inner void. It never works. No matter how much honor a person accumulates, it will not fill that inner vacuum. Instead, it misdirects our life energy away from worthwhile pursuits. If you seek honor, you won't acquire

Torah, because you'll be endlessly preoccupied with egotistical self-glorification, not the real needs of your spiritual life.

Haman, the villain of the Purim story, represents the archetype of one who seeks honor. He had risen in Persian society to be second only to the king in power and prestige. He had wealth and status and all the other perks of office. But his desire for honor knew no limits, and so when he demanded that everyone in the kingdom bow down to him and one person refused, that undid him:

> Then Haman went out that day glad and pleased of heart. But when Haman saw Mordechai in the king's gate and that he did not stand up or tremble before him, Haman was filled with anger against Mordechai. Haman controlled himself, however, went to his house and sent for his friends and Zeresh his wife. Then Haman recounted to them the glory of his riches, and the number of his sons, and every instance where the king had magnified him and how he had promoted him above the princes and servants of the king.[2]

Haman goes on, "And that's not all! Queen Esther invited only me and the king himself to the banquet she prepared for us. And she has invited me to dine with her and the king again tomorrow!"

Does all that he has enumerated give him satisfaction? The next verse drops the boom: "But all this is worth nothing to me as long as I see Mordechai the Jew just sitting there at the palace gate."[3]

His unquenchable appetite for honor proved to be his undoing, and the story ends with him and his ten sons hanging on the gallows.

Honor itself is not a negative trait . . . as long as we are giving it to others. The twenty-four thousand students of Rabbi Akiva who died in the weeks between Passover and Shavuot are said to have died because they did not honor one another.[4] Indeed, rather than seeking it out, honoring others is the way one gains honor for oneself: "Ben Zoma says: 'Who is honored? One who honors others.'"[5]

The cure sounds easy enough—distance yourself from thoughts and activities through which you seek to glorify yourself—but in truth it is very difficult to get free of the desire to be honored. A man once asked the Chassidic teacher Rabbi Simcha Bunim of Peshischa (1765–1827), "Rebbe, I flee from honor, yet it does not pursue me. Where is the truth in the sages' statement that 'One who flees from honor, it pursues him'?" The rebbe replied, "From your question, I can see that when you run from honor, you are looking back over your shoulder to see if it is coming after you. That is not considered fleeing from honor."[6]

Everyone has an ego, and everyone is susceptible to honor seeking. You might think that people who have accomplished little in life would have no basis for seeking honor, but the lack of stellar credits might be just the thing that propels them to run after praise and recognition. As for those who have acquired stores (whether of wisdom or wealth or goods), the more they accomplish in life, including spiritually, the more they may be tempted to seek confirmation of their greatness in the thoughts and words of others.

Rabbi Chaim Shmulevitz (1902–79) often told stories that revealed his struggles with his own appetite for honor. When he was a young and rising star in the yeshiva in Grodno, his teacher, Rabbi Shimon Shkop (1860–1939), would give talks in which he quoted things he had heard from "Rav Chaim." Although everyone knew that Rav Shimon was referring to his own teacher, Rav Chaim Soloveitchik, Rav Chaim Shmulevitz later admitted that he secretly hoped that maybe some uninformed student would think that Rav Shimon was referring to him.

The deep transformation we call acquiring Torah calls for genuine humility. A person who has accomplished much who remains humble and does not seek honor is the most admirable kind of *anav* (humble person). The Talmud says that when Rabbi Yehudah HaNasi passed away, true humility ceased to exist in the world.[7] He had achieved greatness in material wealth, political power, *and* Torah wisdom.[8] Nobody had more to be proud of than he did. But his true greatness shone through in his extreme humility.

Similarly, Rabbi Shlomo Wolbe would not permit the students in his Mussar classes to rise for him when he entered the room or approached the lectern to deliver a talk. He explained that when he spoke in the yeshiva, it was important that the students stand for him, because they had to learn to give honor to the Torah and its teachers. In the Mussar house, however, it was different. There he eschewed honor because he was just "one of them" and not worthy of any special recognition. Others standing, he said, made him feel too important.

The great sixteenth-century kabbalist Rabbi Chaim Vital (1543–1620) agrees with the later Mussar teachers that pursuing honor reflects an inner emptiness.[9] He offers a different way to contend with that sense of being incomplete, which is to be cognizant that one is a small and limited creature whose life is an opportunity to serve a Higher Being. Those who live that sort of life are saved from the perils of conceit and arrogance because they fill the inner self with real substance and do not need to seek external validation.

PRACTICE

Fleeing from honor is not a passive activity. You must actively seek ways to avoid being honored. You need to aspire to humility and make a practice of avoiding situations in which honor is likely to come your way. There is a precedent: In the Talmud, Rabbi Shimon ben Elazar teaches that a sage should travel by the route that will cause the fewest number of people to have to stand in his honor.[10]

As a first step in this practice, identify an area of your life in which you have some real accomplishment, in whatever field, from sports to parenting to academics to creativity. Are you a strong meditator or diligent in prayer? Is there a subject of study that is securely under your belt or a practice you have developed to high level?

Now identify the ways in which people do or might honor you for that achievement.

Finally, resolve to avoid situations in which that honor could be bestowed. Be concrete in determining how you will do that.

The point of this exercise is to acknowledge the truth of your accomplishments and to devise a strategy that will prevent any tendency to seek honor from them, because that weakens your motivation to grow spiritually, and that's what we want to avoid.

לֹא מֵגִיס לִבּוֹ בְּתַלְמוּדוֹ

[35]

Not Being Overly Satisfied in One's Learning

Lo Meigis Libo be'Talmudo

Rabbi Yochanan ben Zakkai used to say, "If you have learned much Torah, do not take credit for yourself, because it is for this that you were created."

—PIRKEI AVOT 2:9

T HE PREVIOUS chapter focused on the pitfalls of seeking to be honored by others; the current teaching turns the focus inward. The concern here is the attitudes we hold toward our own accomplishments.

Good attitudes motivate us to study, practice, and do whatever else is necessary to foster our growth. As we reap the fruit of those good attitudes, however, we start to move into dangerous territory. If we have been diligent, over time our wisdom deepens and the qualities of the soul develop—and perhaps without even noticing it happening, we start to feel quite pleased with ourselves and our progress. As we become comfortable and maybe even a bit complacent, the fire of motivation dies back by almost imperceptible degrees. Sensibilities that gradually corrupt our perspectives and our motivation can then take root in the heart, leading to backsliding, or perhaps even a fall.

The literal meaning of *meigis libo* is "satisfaction" or "satiation of one's heart." There is a dark connotation to the term, however, because when a person is so thoroughly satisfied with his or her accomplishments, it is a very short step to arrogance and condescension. Could someone be arrogant in regard to his or her learning and wisdom? That seems to be just what befell Rabbi Elazar as he rode his donkey back from studying with his teacher.[1] The Talmud tells us explicitly that he was feeling very happy and pleased with himself because he had just learned a great deal of Torah.

As he headed home from his teacher's house, he happened to pass a very ugly person along the road, who greeted him, saying, "Greetings, Rebbe." Rabbi Elazar responded, "Empty one! Are all the people of your town as ugly as you?" The man retorted, "I don't know, but you should go to the Craftsman who made me and tell Him how ugly is the vessel that He made."

Rabbi Elazar instantly realized how wrong he had been. He got off his donkey, prostrated himself before the man, and said, "I have pained you. Forgive me." The man said, "I will not forgive you until you go to the Craftsman who made me and tell Him how ugly is the vessel He made."

The story continues, but the point we need has already been made. We are cautioned to be vigilant against corrupt feelings stealing into our hearts as the twisted outcome of our good efforts to be active, energetic, and successful in our learning and spiritual practice. This is a real hazard on the spiritual path.

This very danger prompts Rabbi Moshe Chaim Luzzatto to caution, "The factor that is responsible more than any other for a person's coming to feel self-important and proud is wisdom."[2]

Ramchal continues, "There is no sage who will not err and will not need to learn from the words of his friends and, very often, even from those of his disciples. How, then, can he pride himself in his wisdom?"

But it happens. In a brief comment in *Duties of the Heart*,[3] Rabbi ibn Paquda lays out the steps that follow once a person starts to feel proud of his or her spiritual accomplishments. He identifies "negative pride" as the condition that arises "when a person is proud of his wisdom, or a righteous person is proud of his deeds, in a way that causes his accomplishments to be great in his eyes; to feel that he can make do with what he has already accomplished; to degrade other people; to look down at the great and wise people of his generation; and to be happy with others' shortcomings."

What we have here is actually a chronology of the steps that ensue once we start to feel pride in our spiritual accomplishments. From those first feelings of self-congratulation, it is a very short step to complacency, which undermines the motivation that is essential to keep moving along the path. Practice falls off, and as we stagnate, spiritual progress slows or grinds to a halt altogether. At that point, rather than give up that enjoyable feeling of pride, we unconsciously seek to build ourselves up by paying careful attention to other people's shortcomings. We become condescending toward others, even those who are in fact greater. Eventually, we not only look down upon others but actually revel in their missteps.

When we pursue a spiritual life, and especially when we experience the changes that are the fruit of our efforts, we need to be on guard for feelings of self-praise and condescension toward others that can come to roost within. There are many cases of even great people who fail in this area. The prophet Jeremiah

(9:23) says it straight out, "Thus says the Lord: 'Let not the wise person glory in his wisdom.'"

Rabbi Yisrael Salanter clearly understood the problem from the roots up. He wrote,[4]

> Do not be surprised that a person with all his faults and smallness of stature nevertheless considers himself greater than his contemporaries. For the more a person loves being praised and admired, the more will his desire for praise grow and cover up his deficiencies, to the point that he no longer senses them. And as the desire to feel that he is better than others grows, his self-admiration heightens the sense of other people's shortcomings. By virtue of his arrogance he will no longer sense other people's virtues and will eventually only be able to sense his own virtues and other people's deficiencies. And so, arrogance will come to fill his entire soul without his even sensing it.

At that point, a person will be living in a world of total falsehood. In truth, there is no justification for self-satisfaction because even a person of knowledge and spiritual accomplishments has achieved so very little. Those who have made the most of every moment of their life and stretched their potential to the maximum, how much will they have learned, and how much real spiritual transformation will they have brought about? The world is so vast, and our achievements are so small! We must be happy—joyful! celebratory!—over whatever we have been able to accomplish, but we must also never allow ourselves to become deluded into feelings of self-satisfaction. Our growth depends on our yearning to learn and grow more.

The hunger and passion to learn and change is the fuel that propels our becoming.

A Torah scholar is called a *talmid chocham*—a *student* who is wise—to emphasize that the path to wisdom is open to one who constantly looks on himself or herself as a student, as one who has so much more room to learn and to grow.

One who seeks to elevate spiritually, who works hard to purify his or her life from the material to the higher realm of the spiritual, must be on guard against the dulling influence of complacency. We need to be vigilantly alert for any signs of being more focused on the ground we have covered than on the path ahead and must regularly renew our fervor for the learning and growth that are our highest purpose.

PRACTICE

In this period, you are bound to have the opportunity to learn something from someone, or to take advice, or you will be asked a question to which you do not know the answer. Be on the lookout for situations like these that reveal the limitations of your own knowledge, expertise, and wisdom; and when you come upon one, embrace that opportunity to be humble and seek to learn from someone else.

You'll learn a great deal, about the subject at hand and about yourself.

אֵינוֹ שָׂמֵחַ בְּהוֹרָאָה

[36]

Not Taking Joy in Handing Down Rulings

Eino Sameach be'Hora'ah

Taking joy in judgments means seeking exposure and fame through the service of God.

—*MIDRASH SHMUEL*

THIS METHOD of personal transformation might seem to apply specifically to judges and rabbis, whose job it is to hand down legal rulings. It certainly does apply to them, but the Talmud teaches that anyone who measures something is a judge,[1] and so we are all judges, in one sense or another. Rabbi Yisrael Salanter explains that words directed at those who preside in courts also apply to every one of us, because we all render all kinds of decisions every day.

Our teaching says we are not to delight in handing down judgments. We are cautioned not to enjoy the exercise of power that is implicit in decision making, because that pleasure can corrupt our judgment. We can end up deciding matters according to our enjoyment, rather than what is best or right.

To issue a legal ruling is a huge responsibility. Many great rabbis let it be known that they were terrified of ruling on matters of Jewish law. The Talmud defines the stakes in a graphic image when it says, "A judge should always view himself as if he had a sword resting between his thighs and Gehinom gapes open below him."[2] If the judge's ruling veers by any degree to the right or the left, there could be dire consequences.

I was once called upon to give an opinion on an issue of Jewish law in which I had some expertise. Orthodox Jewish women wear wigs, and a major source of hair for those wigs is Hindu temples in India, where women often have their heads shaved in preparation for offering worship. It is contrary to Jewish law to take any kind of benefit from idol worship, and here we have a situation in which the wigs might just represent that sort of benefit. It was certainly on the minds of the *beit din* (rabbinic court) in Jerusalem that contacted me, and then on my own mind, as well, that the price of a human hair wig ranges from around $500 to $4,000 and a typical Orthodox woman owns several. A negative ruling would result in thousands of dollars of wigs being thrown out, and businesses disposing of tens of thousands of dollars in inventory. Although that consequence should not have swayed me in providing my understanding of the facts in the issue, nor the *beit din* in making its ruling, knowing what's at stake causes the heart to weigh the matter seriously, taking no pleasure at all in the responsibility.[3]

A rabbinic court is mandated to rule according to the dictates of Torah law. Its decisions are referred to as *hora'ah,* which literally means "teaching." This is the root of the word *Torah* itself. The judges' rulings are, therefore, effectively cast as teaching Torah. Tradition sees contemporary Torah rulings not as innovation but as revealing that which already exists in the Torah but has not yet been uncovered, or "drawn down."

This helps us to appreciate the trepidation over handing down rulings. A judge's decisions are tantamount to writing Torah. How could a judge take lightly or enjoy such a weighty responsibility?

Since a judge's rulings are Torah, nothing in the judgment belongs to or derives from the judge as an individual. The delight we are warned against relates to any feelings of authorship or power one who makes decisions might feel. Those feelings are an indicator that the person is taking too much personal credit and ignoring or minimizing the underlying sources for his or her judgments. If we find ourselves deriving joy from the process of making decisions, especially those of consequence that may have an impact on ourselves and the lives of others, there is a real possibility that the focus has come to fall too much on "me" rather than on the righteousness that ought to be sought in that decision.

The Talmud tells us, "Every judge who judges with complete fairness, even for a single hour, tradition gives that judge credit as though he had become a partner with the Holy Blessed One in the creation of the universe."[4] This teaching provides an important awakening about the impact of our decisions. Every decision we make gives rise to a new situation in the world. If I choose tuna over salmon, tuna becomes a reality and salmon remains an idea in potential. If I speak truth in a situation, there is more truth in the world than had I opted to bolster the side of falsehood. Like that, every decision I make is a contribution to creating the world I live in going forward.

Rav Kook cautions the judge that "defective character traits together with a failure to feel privileged in his public work will cloud his sense of propriety and justice. Instead of values based on an inner sense of justice, his value system becomes relegated to superficial honors."[5] This hearkens back to the quote from the

Midrash Shmuel at the head of this chapter that equates taking joy in making judgments with seeking fame. Rav Kook is actually making a play on words from the Hebrew, relating the word *hora'ah* (teaching, or judgment) to *l'har'ot,* which means to show something or to expose.

The positive things we do are precious not because anybody knows about them, but because they reflect and reveal something true and good. Things done to win recognition are not satisfying, because when the applause dies down, the gnawing emptiness returns. Acting from integrity for the sake of goodness itself is intrinsically satisfying, and that satisfaction lasts. Only such an attitude opens the way for us to connect with our own souls and with God.

Indeed, seeking popularity through the decisions we make could be equated to taking a bribe, since we are motivated more by the reward we'll gain than by concern for the decision itself; and the Torah warns that one who judges must not take bribes.[6] This teaching alerts us to the ways in which our decision making may become biased if it is motivated by anything other than the search for truth, justice, and holiness.

A person who looks within and sees that he or she is drawing enjoyment from sitting in judgment needs to face the fact that his or her spiritual curriculum is making an appearance, and it may be influencing, if not outright corrupting, the decisions being made.

When the exercise of power and wisdom becomes pleasurable, rather than a weighty responsibility, when it is more about serving us than serving God (whose name is Truth), we will inevitably be drawn away from the wise decision making we seek. Truthful, unbiased judgment is an essential element of the transformation that is called acquiring Torah.

PRACTICE

Visualize that you have a razor-sharp sword suspended between your legs. One wrong move to any degree will be very damaging. Spend a few moments holding that image vividly in mind. You might even stand up and walk a few steps with the mental image of the sword between your legs. Be very careful.

If you implant this image firmly enough in your mind through experience (and visualizing is an experience), then it will pop up in your mind when you are about to make a decision, and it will caution you.

That metaphoric sword should not keep you from making decisions, but it ought to help keep you from delighting in being a "judge," one who is entrusted to make rulings.

נושא בעול עם חברו

[37]

Bearing the Burden
with the Other

Noseh ba'Ol im Chaveiro

One day, when Moses had grown up, he went out to his people
and looked on their burdens, and he saw an Egyptian beating a
Hebrew, one of his people. Looking this way and that and seeing no one, he killed the Egyptian and hid him in the sand.

—GENESIS 2:11–12

W E COME now to a primary Mussar practice and one that
defines the distinctiveness of this Jewish spiritual path. So
much of what is called spirituality is focused on your own journey, cultivating your own awareness, being stronger or higher
or better in this way or that. With "bearing the burden with the
other," we turn to face another soul in fulfillment of a major
part of our human purpose. What do you need? How can I help
you bear your burden? No one merits acquiring Torah who does
not hear and respond to that cry.

In the Torah, Joseph asks a simple, human question that
turns out to be the starting point for the entire redemption from

Egypt. When he was in jail and one day saw the faces of his fellow prisoners, the butler and the baker, he asked them, "Why are you looking so sad today?"[1] That question set in motion the chain of events that resulted in Joseph being freed from jail, introduced to the pharaoh, and ultimately appointed as the chief minister who saves Egypt (and the Jewish people) from famine. It all started with being concerned with another's feelings.

The paradigmatic teacher of this trait is Moses. A voice called out from the burning bush and summoned him to lead the Jewish people from exile to revelation. What do we know of Moses's life that earned him this role? The Torah provides us with only a handful of incidents. Raised as a prince in the pharaoh's palace, he "went out" to see the suffering of his people. Then came the incident when he struck down the Egyptian taskmaster who was beating a Jew. As he tried to break up a fight between two Jews, he discovered that others knew of the murder he had committed and he was forced to flee Egypt. Finally, in his exile in Midian, he helped shepherdesses who were being harassed when they tried to water their flocks.

We can only conclude that God called Moses to leadership and destiny because he was the kind of person who cared about other people and who, with every limb of his body, did what he could to help them carry their burdens. This trait is the hallmark of Jewish leadership and greatness.

When God told Moses to free the people from Egypt, Moses asked, "Whom should I tell them sent me?" God responded, *"Ehyeh Asher Ehyeh*—"I will be Who I will be."[2] The Talmud explains this name to mean "I am with them in their present suffering and I will be with them when they suffer under the dominion of other nations."[3] Here is the model we are to follow in interpersonal relations. Pain and suffering cause people to feel isolated and alone. "Bearing the burden" calls on us to penetrate another person's fortress with the aim of relieving that person's pain by joining ourselves to his or her suffering. When visiting a friend whose wife had died, Rabbi Chaim Shmulevitz sat down and wept bitterly over his friend's loss. After twenty minutes, he arose, said traditional words of consolation, and left, having offered the gift of joining himself to his friend's sadness.

Rav Wolbe writes that this is the key to not becoming habituated and dulled in our own spiritual lives.[4] As the years pass and we face the challenges of family, work, and our place in the community, our once-open hearts can become hardened and closed. He says that the vitality of our spiritual lives is commensurate to how much we actually feel and identify with those around us. Our own spiritual growth requires that we help carry the burdens borne by our family, coworkers, communities, and the whole of humanity.

Pay careful attention to the wording of this teaching. It says, "Bearing the burden *with*," not "*for*." We do not acquire Torah and so develop ourselves spiritually through enabling behavior or creating codependency in another person. Each of us must carry our own "yoke," but how good and how satisfying and how human it is to have someone who lends a shoulder to help carry the load.

History tells of many people who did not put themselves first and who gave and sacrificed to help lighten the load another person was bearing. Many such stories emerged from the Holocaust. The life of Rabbi Aryeh Levin (1885–1965), the *tzaddik* of Jerusalem, was all about this practice of bearing the burden with the other.[5] His whole purpose in life was to serve others, and in particular he gave years of his life to being chaplain to the Jewish prisoners of the British administrators of Palestine under the League of Nations Mandate. On his eightieth birthday, those he had helped in prison and their families gathered for a reunion.

When Rav Aryeh stood up to address the crowd, he said, "The importance of this assembly is that it has brought friends together. Moreover, this good meeting is taking place on the other side of the prison bars. . . . It particularly makes my heart glad to see the families of the prisoners, especially the little children, since I have always loved small children." Then he added, "I do not know if I shall be privileged to be with you again like this. All I ask of you is this: Tell your children that there was an old Jew in Jerusalem who loved us so very much!" With that he burst into tears.[6]

When Rabbi Yerucham Levovitz organized the writings of the Alter of Kelm for publication,[7] he placed the pieces on bearing the burden with the other at the beginning because he felt that they were the foundation and the starting point for all Mussar practice. A story about the Alter's son, Nachum Zeev, puts the whole of this practice into clear focus through a simple anecdote. He once visited a student in the hospital. The student bemoaned the fact that his roommate, who was a Jew, was eating the hospital food. Rav Nachum Zeev advised the student, "You should feel for the pain of the fellow who has had a limb amputated and be less concerned with his non-kosher diet."

This one practice is so fundamentally valuable because when you take it on, your entire personal spiritual curriculum is revealed to you. In *Pirkei Avot* 1:14, Hillel asks, "If I am not for myself, who will be for me? But when I am only for myself, what am I?"

PRACTICE

Listen! Whose cry do you hear? Listen! You can hear it. You know whom I mean. Will you reach out to help that person carry his or her burden? Will you help lift the yoke he or she bears?

Rabbi Reuven Leuchter is a student of Rav Wolbe who advocates using visualizations, as taught by the Alter of Kelm. Visualizing helps bring others' pain (or joy) to life within us, much more than any news report can ever do. The more details we conjure up in our mind's eye, the closer we will experience another's pain or joy.

Think of someone who is close to you who is in some form of pain today. It could be physical or emotional pain. It could be the sadness of loss or the anxiety of uncertainty. Illness, failure, abandonment, loneliness . . . there are innumerable sources of suffering.

Once you have identified that person, close your eyes and visualize his or her experience from the inside. Depending on the source of the pain, bring that experience to life within you, in your own imagination. Take the time and make the effort to visualize the details of the situation, because the poignancy and the reality of another person's feelings often lie in the small things. Make your inner experience as vivid and intense as your mind will allow, and, as you exercise your imagination in this way, let the other person's pain become your pain.

Reach out to that person. Taking caring action is the fruit and fulfillment of this practice.

מכריעו לכף זכות

[38]

Judging Others Favorably

Machri'o le'Chaf Zechut

As she kept praying to the Lord, Eli observed her mouth. Hannah was praying in her heart and her lips were moving but her voice was not heard. Eli thought she was drunk and said to her, "How long are you going to stay drunk? Put away your wine." "Not so, my lord," Hannah replied. "I am a woman who is deeply troubled. I have not been drinking wine nor beer; I was pouring out my soul to the Lord."

—GENESIS 18:1–3

IT SEEMS WE are all judges, passing sentence on everyone we meet for how they talk, what they wear, who they sit with. We're being told here to develop a positive eye and not to be so critical. We are to give others the benefit of the doubt, and there's good reason for that, if only because our conclusions are so often mistaken. How often do we decide with instant clarity that someone is lazy, only to find out that they suffer from arthritis? Or that someone has had too much to drink, when, in fact, they recently suffered a stroke?

Are you as prone to jump to conclusions as I am? I seem to

have an involuntary reflex to form a judgment, even when I don't have all the facts. And I tend to lean toward the side of indictment. To excuse myself a bit, I think this is a feature of human nature. It wouldn't be so bad if only I weren't wrong so much of the time. More generally, though, most of us tend to have a general outlook that is critical, and here we are being guided to cultivate a positive view of life, especially in regard to other people. Negative judgment separates us from other people and closes our hearts to them, making it impossible to develop the love and closeness we want and need.

You send an e-mail or leave a voicemail asking someone to get back to you, and days go by without a reply. Don't people have family emergencies that take precedence over emails?

Your friend keeps kosher, and you see him coming out of a non-kosher restaurant wiping his hands. Isn't the need for a bathroom sometimes urgent?

You confide in someone and watch as she goes directly to talk to the one person you'd especially like not to know what you just said. Don't people talk about all sorts of things, not necessarily your secrets?

The scenarios are endless. Our tendency is to assign guilt and to condemn without even considering any alternative—especially innocent—possibility. That we are so often wrong in our assessments of others is enough reason to tilt the balance (of our judgment) to the side of merit. And, indeed, the phrase *machrio l'chaf zechut* literally means "to tilt the balance to the side of merit."

Maybe it is ironic that people who are striving to grow spiritually are especially susceptible to slipping into a negative outlook. Rav Wolbe identifies becoming critical of others as one of the major pitfalls of spiritual growth. It may be necessary to examine our own shortcomings as we pursue our spiritual path, and as we do that, we are prone to becoming critical of others. Spiritual growth should foster humility and love, but too often it fuels arrogance and condescension. We need to train ourselves in the opposite tendency. If negative judgment is human nature, we need to teach and condition ourselves to give the benefit of the doubt.

We're given an image of the ideal in a story in the Talmud that tells of a worker who was employed far from his home.[1] After three years, he told his boss that he wanted to be paid up for his services, so he could return to his family. His boss replied that he had nothing with which to pay him. The worker went home empty-handed and sad but without complaining.

Later, the employer showed up at the worker's home with loads of fine things to compensate for the man's wages. He asked the employee, "When I said I had no money, what did you think?" "I thought you had used your wealth to buy merchandise," the worker replied. "And when I said, I don't have any animals to give you, what did you think?" "That they were rented to others," answered the employee. And so for each possible form of payment, the employee testified that he had not jumped to a negative judgment.

"You were correct in every case," said the boss, "but today I am able to pay you." And then he blessed his worker, saying, "Just as you judged me favorably, so may the Lord judge you favorably."

So significant is this practice that many count judging others favorably as one of the 613 biblical commandments, based on the verse "Judge your friend righteously,"[2] which is interpreted to refer not only to judges in a court of law but also to each of us in our daily lives.

Even as you work on aspects of yourself where you could do better, make an effort to judge others favorably and to give them the benefit of the doubt. See yourself as a student who has so much more to accomplish, not someone who has "risen" above others. Look to the positive in others, and then extend that experience into your life in general.[3] That way, you will become a positive and loving person, and that is surely a sign of spiritual practice that has gone right.

We learn a practical tip on how to tilt the balance of judgment toward the positive from the other place, a variant of the phrase that features in this teaching shows up, in *Pirkei Avot* 1:6. In that case, the teaching is *"Hevei dan et kol ha'adam l'khaf zechut,"* which translates as "Give everyone the benefit of the doubt." But the phrase *"kol ha'adam,"* which is usually translated as "everyone," can also mean "the whole person." Irving Bunim points out that if you take into account the whole person, in his or her entirety, you are bound to find that there are redeeming features that ought to factor in, and maybe even displace, your impulsive negative judgments.[4]

Our efforts to grow spiritually should not lead us to trample on the people around us. Our lives must always be infused with spreading love and friendship, and not the opposite, because, ultimately, that is what spiritual growth is supposed to do.

PRACTICE

We come naturally to being judgmental, but it takes a good deal of effort to develop a good eye. With that in mind, bring someone to mind about whom you tend to have a negative assessment. You don't like this person; you don't like what he or she does or how. Maybe this person even did something wrong in some way.

Now for the hard part—it's your mission to find at least one good quality in this person.

Here's an extreme example. A man who was on trial for killing another man admitted he did it and explained the circumstances. Apparently, he had tracked his victim for days to assess his daily habits, seeking the right time to do the deed. He observed that his victim walked his child to school every morning, so the killer ruled that out as a time to shoot him, because, as he said in court, he certainly was not the kind of person who would assassinate someone in front of children.

Think about that for a moment. Surely, we are entitled to judge such a dastardly person negatively. But is he without virtue?

Now think closer to home. Whom do you dislike, even with good reason? Is that person also without virtue? Identify at least one good quality in that person.

As a way to extend this practice beyond a simple thought exercise, place something distinctive in a pocket you can easily reach with your hand. It could be a pebble, a large coin, or something like that. When you become aware that judgment is coming into your mind, reach into your pocket to touch what you have placed there. Let that remind you to give the benefit of the doubt.

מעמידו על האמת

[39]

Leading Others to Truth

Ma'amido al ha'Emet

Rabban Shimon ben Gamliel would say: "The world stands on
three things: justice, truth, and peace."

—PIRKEI AVOT 1:18

TRUTH IS SAID to be the seal of God,[1] and dedication to
truth is a sign of wisdom and spiritual maturity. It is obvious, and we all know how much harm comes about because of
lying and other forms of falsehood. Yet what we see in this, our
thirty-ninth focus for acquiring Torah, is that just being truthful
with people is actually not enough. For the heart to blossom, it
goes without saying that we must act and speak with allegiance
to truth, but we learn here that we must also take responsibility
to "set *others* into truth," which is a literal translation of our text.

In recent chapters, we've been exploring the responsibility
the seeker holds to share the burdens of others, and now we
learn that bringing them toward truth is part of that task. When
you guide people toward their ethical center and to adopt perspectives that are grounded in reality, you help them establish a
solid foundation on which to build a life that is not marred by

the errors of ignorance or illusion. Doing that for others is a necessary part of our own spiritual practice.

That lesson is carried by a story in the Talmud.[2] The sage Rava was being vexed by his wife. If he asked her to make lentils, she made peas. If he asked her to make peas, she made lentils. When his son Chiya got older, he (Chiya) would reverse the request so that his mother would inadvertently make just what his father wanted. Rava said to his son, "Things are going better with your mother." Chiya confessed, "I am reversing it for her." Rava said, "You should not do this, as the verse says, 'They have taught their tongue to speak lies and weary themselves to commit iniquity.'[3]"

Commentators wonder why Rava tells his son to stop. After all, it is an accepted principle that one is permitted to divert from the truth for the sake of peace.[4] Rabbeinu Yonah answers by explaining that a person should avoid lying even when it is permitted, or about inconsequential matters, because there is a danger of developing the habit of falsehood, which might then open the doors to lying about important things. Rava was wise enough to recognize that, even though Chiya's lying was serving his own interests well, he had an obligation to lead his son to truth.

When we see someone do or say something we believe to be wrong, they have veered from the truth, and it is our responsibility—not only to them but also to our own spiritual growth—to help them find their way back to truth. That sort of response to someone else's mistake is not what comes naturally to us. Left to be guided by our own lower nature, our tendency is to take pleasure in somebody else's error. This is such a deep-seated inclination. Do you remember being a child in school and how the class reacted when someone answered a question with an outrageously incorrect response? Do you recall the giddy delight among the students, how everyone keeled over laughing? But do you also remember how mortified the erring student was? How red did he or she blush? And then blanch? And cry? Or run and hide?

It isn't fitting for an adult to make a show of delight when someone else trips up, even though inside that adult there may well lurk a grade school child who is still snickering and pointing at the one who slipped.[5] We need to aspire to something higher than indulging that gleeful sense of superiority we are tempted to frolic in when someone else makes a mistake. That behavior is not the way of someone who seeks holiness.

The better response to someone's error is to teach them. That approach is consistent with Jewish values, which tell us that we have a responsibility to look out for other people. "You shall not stand by the blood of your neighbor," says Leviticus 19:16. In its simplest interpretation, the verse refers to avenging murder. But the rabbis point to the role blood plays when someone is embarrassed. They refer to embarrassment as *malbish panim,* which literally means "whitening of the face,"[6] and they liken the pallor of embarrassment to the bloodless face of the dead. Not mockery, not humiliation, but taking someone by the hand and teaching them ought to be our response to someone else's misstep.

This is what is meant by "lead others to truth." That injunction does not give us license to be judgmental or to bully or even to be sure that our way is the right way. The task is *to lead* and we will only be able to accomplish that goal by being sensitive, patient, humble, and caring in the way of a good and effective teacher, not self-righteous or intimidating. Rabbi Samson Raphael Hirsch explained that a leader should be prepared to speak out against injustice and take a stand for truth, even if it is unpopular; but the leader should not force his or her views upon others. We have a responsibility to lead others by teaching them, as we learn from the fact that the most common title applied to the greatest of Jewish leaders, Moses, is not "Moses our leader" but rather "Moses our teacher" (*Moshe Rabbeinu*).

When the moon is first seen at the beginning of the month, the blessing of *Birkat HaLevana* is recited. In that blessing, we say that the moon acts with "truth." Rabbi Yisrael Salanter helps us to understand what that means by defining truth as being when something follows the path for which it was intended without veering to either side.[7] Similarly, Rava Shlomo Wolbe writes,[8]

The most basic parameter of truth is consistency. This classification does not only refer to a discrepancy between knowledge, awareness and reality, but also that there not be contradictions *within a person's essential nature.* [Emphasis mine.]

This definition provides us with a way to appreciate what is involved in leading others to truth. When we realize that truth means following a consistent path in life with no contradictions within a person's essential nature, then we learn that the practice of *leading others to truth* calls on us to make an effort to bring others to *their* truth, to assist them to realize *their* potential on their terms, to teach them how to live their lives in ways that have integrity and are consistent with the unique and individual divine image in which they are fashioned.

PRACTICE

Identify someone in your life whom you think is veering from the truth, as you understand and appreciate it. That could be someone who seems to be making a decision or taking a path you think is based on falsehood or illusion. Or someone who seems quite deluded, or may be acting according to values you feel not to be true, for example.

Think how you might lead that person to truth. Give careful thought to what it would take to show effective leadership because there are many strategies that may just not do the trick, such as confronting or criticizing.

If you feel you have a strategy that has a reasonable chance of redirecting that person toward truth, try it. You owe it to them, and, since we are talking here about your own acquisition of Torah, you owe it to yourself, as well.

מעמידו על השלום

[40]

Leading Others to Peace

Ma'amido al ha'Shalom

Turn from evil and do good; seek peace and pursue it.

—PSALMS 34:14

*P*IRKEI AVOT 1:12 advises us, "Hillel said: 'Be of the disciples of Aharon, loving peace and pursuing peace.'" We all want peace, and we pray for peace. What can we learn about peace from Aharon, brother of Moses?

Aharon was the *kohen gadol,* the high priest. He was the focal religious figure for the whole nation, and it was his task to connect every segment of the people into a single and united whole. Division and enmity were inimical to national unity, so he had to work hard to minimize the forces of conflict and division and maximize the forces of peace and harmony.[1]

As mentioned in an earlier chapter, the Hebrew word for peace—*shalom*—shares its linguistic root with the word *shalem,* which means "whole" and even "perfect." Peace is the outcome of having brought all the components of a situation to a condition of wholeness, and that is what Aharon did—forging a disparate and fractious people into a single unit. From this

215

perspective, we see that peace is much more than an absence of conflict. Oppressed people may not take up arms, but it takes more than a lack of fighting to create peace. Real peace flows from wholeness, and only when we bring about a unification of the parts, do we achieve true peace.

From this perspective, peace is not its own goal but a by-product and an index of having done what is necessary to repair or bring wholeness to a situation. The prophet Zechariah, in verse 8:19, says, "You shall love truth and peace." Not peace alone, because peace without truth will not endure. If we want real peace, we have to pursue it via the route of working for justice, truth, and repair.

Our current teaching talks not about achieving peace in our own lives but rather about "leading others to peace," reiterating the theme we encountered in the last chapter, when we were told that our own spiritual growth requires that we lead others to truth. In the Jewish view, the journey toward holiness requires that we think and act beyond our own immediate circumstances to help bring well-being to those around us. In this case, the lesson is that your own spiritual growth depends on you reaching out and taking action to lead others to peace. Anyone committed to spiritual growth should not be satisfied to enjoy peace in the small circumference of his or her own life while others are living in distress.

Leading people in the direction of peace means encouraging them to see objectively and acknowledge what is broken in a relationship and then helping them fix that broken piece. That means helping them grasp which aspects of a situation need to be made whole, and helping them bring those factors to completion. We have a role to play in helping others make their relationships—whether in the family or in the community, workplace, or nation—whole (*shalem*), so that peace (*shalom*) emerges from the wholesome unification of parts.

This is not an easy task. When there is conflict or brokenness in a relationship, the situation is always complex, and it is difficult to sort out who has responsibility for what. Yet that is exactly what needs to happen, because wholeness (hence peace) can only come about when each party takes ownership of his or her own contribution to the problem and does something about it. In leading others to peace, we begin by encouraging our friends not just to avoid blaming each other, but also to find the humility to examine whether something in their attitude or behavior might merit attention in order that the broken can be made whole.

In the Friday night prayers we find the phrase *ufros aleinu sukkat shelomecha*—"Spread over us the shelter [*sukkah*] of Your peace." Rav Dessler asks, "What does the *sukkah,* the temporary hut we build each year on the festival of Sukkot, have to do with peace?"[2] He answers by pointing out that when we leave the comfort and security of our homes and move into a makeshift hut, that process is meant to humble us, to bring us to experience the vulnerability that is our true situation, even if it is largely invisible to us at any given moment. That experience brings us to humility, and humility is a precondition for establishing the wholeness that breeds peace.

Being humble opens the door to peace, but this is no pacifist creed. The oft-quoted verse Ecclesiastes 3:8 reminds us, "There is a time for war and a time for peace." The Talmud and Jewish law tell us that there are circumstances in which arguing, fighting, and even war are justified, but only according to a crucial criterion: The conflict must be *l'shem shamayim*—literally "in the name of heaven." Action that is *l'shem shamayim* has no ulterior motive and no ego involved. It is always for a higher purpose, which means not for the sake of self-interest. Conflicts that are *l'shem shamayim* have the potential to lead to peace. Arguments and fights that are not in the name of heaven may end in victory for one side and a cessation of hostilities but will not likely give rise to wholeness and true and lasting peace.

The Torah is very concerned with peaceful relations and places at the top of such unions the category of covenant. Rabbi Jonathan Sacks describes the nature of a covenant: "This . . . supreme form of relationship is one that does not depend on power, superior force, or dominant-submissive hierarchy. In a covenantal relationship both parties respect the dignity of the other. A covenant exists only in virtue of freely given consent."[3]

When the Torah refers to the act of forging covenants, the phrase it uses is *kritut brit*. The verb *kritut* literally means "to cut." A covenant is the coming together of two parties in a binding relationship, so why would the Torah use the seemingly contradictory image of cutting to refer to such an agreement? The Vilna Gaon explains that the only way an everlasting covenant can be formed is if each party is willing to give up— or, to "cut away"—a piece of himself or herself for the sake of the other. That cutting away opens the possibility of creating a new entity made whole by the covenant between the two parties.

The peace we seek—and toward which we need to lead others—is a true peace that is based on humility, truth, selflessness, integrity, and wholeness. Psalms 34:15 tells us to "Seek peace and pursue it." Peace can be elusive and must be actively chased to be realized. This method of transformation calls on us to take the initiative to help others to make this effort.

PRACTICE

Think through a conflict involving someone you care about. What could you "cut away" from your own side to make that person willing to resolve the issue in a manner that preserves the integrity of the parties involved, and also brings about real peace?

Might it be something related to your own ego?

What initiative and effort could you take to help create wholeness and peace in this situation?

מתישב לבו בתלמודו

[41]

Being Settled in One's Studies

Mityashev Libo be'Talmudo

Decisions call for clarity of mind, like the sky on a day when the north wind blows.

—*ERUVIN 65A*

J EWISH WAYS of spirituality and growth always involve some study, but not as texts are studied in secular settings. Jewish learning is a ritualized process that is as much a spiritual discipline as it is a method for gaining knowledge. For centuries, students have read and then questioned and argued—among themselves, with teachers—seeking to understand and absorb material for the sake of learning and to reap the transformative potential embedded in the process.

The word *mityashev* comes from the linguistic root that means "settled." A house of Torah study is called a *yeshiva* (from the same root), because it is meant to be a dwelling place for study, not just a classroom where people come to learn. Spiritual practice is not like a hobby or something we do occasionally or on the side. Rather, it ought to be where we *live,* while everything else in our life is where we visit.

At the time when Rav Chaim Volozhin established the yeshiva in Volozhin (which was the prototype of all modern-day yeshivot), students were referred to as *talmidei yeshiva*—"students of the yeshiva." Rav Chaim changed that to be *b'nei yeshiva*—"children of the yeshiva." This is still the way we refer to yeshiva students today. Even after they leave that place to take jobs and raise families, they are considered to have grown up in that yeshiva home, and so they are still children of the yeshiva.

Study is an essential practice for a person walking the transformative path of Mussar, because over the centuries, wise ancestors have observed human life and recorded their findings, and studying the texts they have left to us gives us insight into our own lives. Would we be able to come up with our own accurate understanding of humility? On our own, would we see how humility is connected to anger? Or the connection of anger to sorrow?[1] There is much to learn from those who have gone this way before us, and we absorb those lessons through study.

Take, for example, patience, which is a feature of the inner life we experience every day, though more often in its absence, as impatience. Do you have a clear understanding of what actually constitutes patience? Some people would say that patience is an unflappable inner calm that permits a person to wait for or be diverted from his or her goals almost indefinitely, without any emotional turmoil. Others would say that patience is the ability to contain feelings and not act out when provoked and emotionally reactive. Which is it? Is patience a kind of equanimity, or is it forbearance under stress?

When we look at the Mussar literature, we see that the Jewish view of patience endorses only the latter understanding. The Hebrew word for patience is *savlanut,* which is related to two other words with intersecting meanings: *sevel,* which means "suffering," and *sabal,* which means "a porter," the person who carries your bags at the train station or airport. This study reveals that being patient involves bearing the burden of your own emotional suffering. It has nothing to do with being unflappable, though we wouldn't know that without studying the lessons that have been bequeathed to us by previous generations.

Studying Mussar texts provide a lens of a thousand years of wisdom through which we can perceive our own inner lives more clearly. We need effective techniques to gain access to those lessons, and our current method for acquiring Torah provides a major guideline when it tells us that we should study in a *settled* way.

Being "settled in one's studies" means making study "fixed" and not haphazard. There are several kinds of "settling" that are essential to a successful learning process:

Settle on the subject. There is no end to the number of things you can dip into in the ocean of Jewish texts and even texts just from the Mussar tradition, and you will never be able to study them all. What's your priority? What's your goal? Consider carefully what you choose to study because you may be embarking on a process that will keep you engaged for years.

Settle on a partner. It is always better to study with a partner than on your own. A partner brings different perspectives and causes you to see things through different eyes. As well, when you study with a partner, you become accountable to someone else, and that is very helpful for disciplining your study. The person you choose to study with needs to be compatible in as many ways as possible, yet being different from each other in some ways can add spice and interest to your studies. You want someone who is reliable, who is interested in the same fields as you, and who complements rather than duplicates you. I try to find partners for myself who have skills or expertise that I lack and who might, in turn, appreciate my strengths, which they may not possess.

Settle on a schedule—and stick to it. Being consistent in learning is as crucial to the practice as is being regular in exercise and hygiene. Be regular in the time you meet to study and just as consistent in where you do your learning. The fewer variables you introduce into the system, the fewer holes into which your practice can fall.

Settle your mind. *Yishuv da'at* was an earlier method we studied (chapter 12), which focused on mental calmness, and the word *yishuv* and the *mityashev* that we find here come from the same root. Of course, you need a settled mind to study. You also need to be committed and resolute in your determination to study. The more you are a determined student, the more success you will have in the acquisition of Torah, with all that entails.

Being settled in these ways will free your mind from unnecessary agitation and uncertainty, and you will see the results in the quality and depth of what you gain from your learning.

When Rabbi Yisrael Salanter initiated the Mussar movement in Lithuania in the mid-nineteenth century, he organized groups of laypeople, especially from among the Torah-educated and pious, "for the study of Mussar texts, such as *Path of the Just* and *Duties of the Heart,* with keen concentration and fervor. Somewhat later, when a number of these individuals had become fervent Mussar adherents, he founded his first Mussar *shtiebel* [house],"[2] where his disciples and followers would come to learn, practice, and grow.

A typical study session in a Mussar house was divided into two parts. First, the student looked into a text, and in the second part, the student engaged in active, contemplative practice to internalize and apply the lessons learned from the wisdom of the tradition.[3] The foundation, we can see, was the text study, done in a settled way.

PRACTICE

What are the primary commitments to which you give your time? How essential are your studies in the overall layout of your life? Do you fix your spiritual commitments on your calendar and work other activities around your spiritual life, or do you try to eke out a minute here or there for your spirituality, when your real priorities lie elsewhere?

To make that question specific and practical, do you have a regular partner with whom you study? If not, you should, and if so, can you find another hour a week for learning? I can't praise highly enough the gift tradition has given us by passing down to us this process of studying, along with its benefits.

Is there someone in your community whom you could approach to study with you? Could a rabbi or teacher make a match for you?

There are more options than there are excuses not to get learning. Calmly and with patience and with a settled mind, of course.

שואל כענין

[42]

Asking Pertinent Questions

Shoel ke'Inyan

The shy person does not learn.

—PIRKEI AVOT 2:5

OF ALL THE Jewish festivals, Passover is the most widely observed. The Bible designates Passover as one of the three pilgrimage festivals when all adult Jewish men were to travel to Jerusalem. Throughout the generations, the Passover meal in the home has often been a focal event on the annual family calendar, even among Jews who are not very observant of tradition. Passover derives its importance from the fact that it commemorates the freeing of the Israelites from Egyptian slavery and their flight from Egypt over 3,000 years ago, marking the birth of the Jewish people.

The central ritual of Passover taking place at the family table involves a young child asking a specified set of questions (known as the "four questions") of the family elder who is leading the evening ritual, beginning with "Why is this night different from all other nights?"

But what if there is no young child to ask the questions? The rabbis anticipated that situation in the Talmud, where they wrote that if there is no child who can ask, the man's wife should ask the questions. If she can't do it, then he should ask them of himself. "Even two scholars who are well versed in the laws of Passover ask one another."[1]

The "four questions" are not the only way that questioning is built into in the Passover rituals. Right near the beginning of the meal, all participants are to wash their hands but, unlike any other instance of ritual handwashing, in this case no blessing is said. The rabbis explain that the reason no blessing follows the washing is so that the children will notice the difference and that will prompt them to ask about it. There really isn't an answer to the question; the goal is to get the young ones into the frame of mind to be asking questions.

Several other practices were instituted that also were meant to encourage children to question, including removing the food from the table, as if the meal was over, and dipping vegetables twice. The rabbis understood how important it is to ask questions. They recognized that questioning leads to discussion, interaction, clarification, learning, and memory, and they believed that a tradition of questioning would endure more than a tradition of dogma. Two thousand years later, they seem to have been correct.

It is a characteristic aspect of Jewish spiritual practice that the "faithful" are encouraged to ask and to probe every aspect of belief and practice. Indeed, anyone who has spent time in a yeshiva or has participated in Talmud study can testify that the student who asks the best question is the one who is praised the most. A story in the Talmud about Rabbi Yochanan tells of him demoting to the back row of the study hall a student who asked no questions, and then promoting that same student to the front row when he began to ask.[2] We measure a scholar's stature not solely by the answers he gives but also by the questions he poses. The poet Shlomo ibn Gabirol (1021–58) captures this idea in his saying "The question of a wise man is half of wisdom."[3] He also said, "The finest quality of man is that he should be an inquirer."[4]

Although rooted in the tradition of Talmud study, questioning has permeated every aspect of Jewish culture. Dr. Isidor Rabi, who won the Nobel Prize for Physics in 1944, attributed his decision to become a research scientist to the way his mother greeted him after school. "My mother made me a scientist. Every other Jewish mother in Brooklyn would ask her child after school: 'So? Did you learn anything today?' Not my mother. She always asked me a different question. 'Izzy,' she would say, 'did you ask a good question today?' That difference made me a scientist."[5]

Questioning is so integral to Jewish culture as to be worthy of a joke: "Tell me, is it true that Jews always answer a question with a question?" To which the answer is, "Who told you that?"

I have heard it said that God loves stories, and Jews love questions.

We are encouraged to question because we have nothing to fear and everything to gain. Our task is to clarify and illuminate Truth, and the best way to do that is through asking questions, so that our uncertainties and misunderstandings can be brought into the open, where they can be addressed. This approach characterizes Torah study but is also the way to go in all areas of spirituality. Even if we have made great strides in our spiritual lives, the moment we stop asking questions, the moment we stop reexamining our assumptions, our learning, our practices, we put a stop to the growth process. Growth demands the inner strength and conviction to be constantly asking, to probe deeper, and to seek new avenues to rise higher.

When we place ourselves within the flow of questioning and

answering that has been bubbling through the Jewish world for millennia, we sharpen our minds to be able to analyze, learn, and grow. We are encouraged to take nothing for granted nor to accept matters on faith as dogma. The real answers we seek come from the real questions we ask.

There are, in fact, two different words for *question* in Hebrew, and each carries a different sensibility. A *she'elah* is a quest for information, whereas a *kushya* is a challenge, reflecting the difference between an ordinary question and one involving a difficulty that has no obvious solution. By asking a *she'alah,* a person seeks to fill in their factual understanding, whereas a *kushya* questions the truth or authority of a statement. Knowing which kind of question to ask, and asking it in the right way, requires training and effort. We have to learn how to ask questions with the purpose of drawing out truth and not as a way of disproving or arguing for the sake of arguing or, worse still, as a way to ridicule or mock or to glorify ourselves. There is a way to ask a question that reveals the very foundation upon which things are built.

Won't we be diminished in the eyes of our partners (or students? or self?) if we say, "I don't understand what this means." "How can that make sense?" "Do you follow what she is saying?" The right way to inquire is with humility and a commitment to clarifying and seeking knowledge. Despite the fact that absolute clarity in wisdom and in life is ultimately beyond us, it is still incumbent upon us to continue to ask. Hopefully, our teachers and our partners will appreciate our questions, but even if that does not happen, the questions need to be asked. Questions are wedges that pry open hearts and minds to all that the tradition has to offer us. "We are closer to God when we are asking questions than when we think we have the answers," said Rabbi Abraham Joshua Heschel.[6]

There is a story in the Talmud that tells of a prankster who tries to get Hillel to lose his temper by asking provocative questions.[7] Each time he asks why Babylonians have round heads or why the feet of the Africans are wide, Hillel begins his response with, "My child, you have asked a great question." The Talmud praises Hillel for his forbearance. In the end, Hillel encourages, "Ask all the questions you have to ask." He so appreciated that questions are the key to the learning process. And so should we.

PRACTICE

What have you been thinking about recently that could be framed as a question? Is it something about the soul? An inner trait? Shabbat? Jewish approaches to current events? How to bake challah? Why a mezuzah is always affixed to the doorpost at an angle? What to study next?

Frame a question.

Now decide to whom you will take your question. A friend? A teacher? An expert in the field?

My child,[8] now ask your great question.

שומע ומוסיף

[43]

Listening and Contributing

Shomea u'Mosif

Let the wise listen and add to their learning.

—PROVERBS 1:5

AT THE TIME that I first met my Mussar teacher, Rabbi Yechiel Yitzchok Perr, in 1999, I was like an empty vessel.[1] He had all the knowledge and depth in Mussar, and I was a lost soul seeking guidance. Our first meeting lasted six hours, and in that time he poured from his well into my waiting ears. I listened and absorbed. It would not have crossed my mind at that time to think that one day I would write books and add to this tradition I was hungry to receive. And yet I have done that because what follows from deep listening and understanding is an obligation to add one's own teaching to the stream of tradition. That's what keeps it from running dry.

The first part of this injunction is to listen. We need to be sure that we have listened and absorbed what someone is saying to us or what has already been said about a topic. We were told the importance of listening very early on in this process, as the second method of acquiring Torah. There we distinguished be-

230

tween hearing and listening. Hearing is the first encounter with an idea or teaching; once heard, the idea needs to be studied, explored, and developed in order that it can be appreciated and absorbed in your heart. That's the sort of listening we need to practice.

Jewish law prohibits gossip, and I frequently find that when I teach that rule, somebody objects to defend gossip, contending that it has a positive social function because it is a sharing of information that binds people together. I don't argue; I just invite the person to join me in going deeper in exploring the laws of speech that have been developed within the Jewish tradition. I want the person to understand that Jewish law is not primarily concerned with whether the information is true, with whether the person might say the same thing themselves, or with whether it is new information, but rather with the harm the words might cause. Only once students come to appreciate that being cautious about doing harm is the main issue do they have the foundation to understand the different values that motivate this Jewish ethical principle. I have to help them "listen" to what has been said previously, so they can approach their own reality in an informed way.

Listening like that is a good process in its own right, but the current teaching links listening to "contributing" or "adding." This second part is actually problematic. It seems to stand in direct contradiction to what is written in the Torah itself, where we read, "Everything that I command you, you shall be careful to do it. You shall neither add to it nor subtract from it."[2] How, then, can we add? What are we entitled to contribute?

Indeed, some Torah scholars have answered this question by saying, "Nothing!" Rabbi Eliezer was once asked some thirty questions dealing with the festival of Sukkot but answered only half of them.[3] It wasn't that he did not have the answers to all of them, but he refused to say anything that he had not heard from his own teacher. People asked him, "Is it true that you never say anything unless you heard it from your teacher?" To which Rabbi Eliezer replied, "You are causing me to say something which I never heard from my teacher!"

Rabbi Chaim Shmulevitz was troubled by this story. We know from elsewhere in the Talmud that Rabbi Eliezer did, in fact, teach new ideas that had not been expressed before. Rabbi Shmulevitz explains that Rabbi Eliezer could "add" in this way because he was such a diligent student of his own teacher and thought through his new ideas so carefully that he was confident that, had his own teacher been presented with the issue at hand, he would have responded exactly as Rabbi Eliezer had done.

Rabbi Eliezer thus models for us that we all need to add our own contribution to wisdom, but we prepare ourselves to be able to do that by listening to what came beforehand. Absorbing what we learn from others is how we build a foundation for our own thought. And then we must add. Each of us has unique life experience and our own wisdom to contribute to the world.

The Maharal points out that a natural source, one whose waters flow from itself, is referred to as a "living spring."[4] The living spring replenishes itself from within. Rav Aryeh Leib Heller (1745–1812)[5] adds to this image by telling us that in heaven the soul is compared to a well (whose waters are filled from another source). The soul is sent down to this world to become a living spring that flows with creative potential. The essence of life flows from within oneself, adding to what already is, and then being replenished anew from within.

But how are we to contribute? Are we supposed to invent our own novel ideas? Are we looking to come up with something that has never been seen or said before? And how does adding to what we learn help us transform ourselves and blossom?

The Vilna Gaon starts us toward answering these questions by saying, "Novel interpretation of Torah is everything that is learned more and clarified more within us. It is each time one involves oneself in the words of Torah and discovers a deeper taste."[6]

His point is that one should not set out to fabricate some spanking new idea that has never before been thought or said, but rather to seek to *understand* in one's own unique way— deeper and deeper. The point is to cause one's studies to penetrate to the core of being, there to unlock the potential that lies within each of us.

One implication of this teaching is that even one who transmits what he or she has learned should not be just a mouthpiece for received ideas. It's not enough to listen and repeat; one must contribute, as well. Abraham's servant Eliezer is credited in the Talmud for faithfully teaching the lessons he learned from Abraham,[7] but he is said to have failed to contribute his own understanding, and thus he failed to make the Torah a part of his essential makeup—the Torah passed through him as if he simply filled a bucket with water and then dumped it out to others without the addition of anything originating in his own inner self. Nor did any residue remain with him.

The beginning of this method of transformation is to master the art of listening faithfully and enthusiastically so we absorb the lessons made available to us by our teachers. But that is only the beginning. We must then work to integrate the message within us so we come *to understand it in our unique way.* When we offer that understanding to others, our teaching will embody our individuality and will actualize the enormous possibility that lies in potential within us. That's how our study comes alive within us and through us, for others.

PRACTICE

Identify an area of your life (or the life of someone close to you) in which a decision is needed. There will undoubtedly be Jewish law that is relevant to that decision, so I invite you to do yourself the favor of reviewing that law ("listening") before you make (or advise the person to make) the decision ("contributing").

In fact, you may need to do that "listening" in a literal way, because you may need the help of a rabbi to identify where the relevant material on law is to be found. Asking for help is a good way to set up the listening you need to do.

לומד על מנת ללמד

[44]

Learning in Order to Teach

Lomed al menat le'Lamed

Rabbi Yochanan said: "One who studies the Torah but does not teach it is like a myrtle in the wilderness whose fragrance is wasted."

—ROSH HASHANA 23A

STUDY HELPS us grow and transform, because there were wise people in previous generations from whom we can learn. But why shouldn't we do our learning for its own sake (and our sake) rather than in order to teach others?

One answer is that there is a verse in the Torah that simply commands, "You shall teach [these words] to your children."[1] In the same vein, Rabbi Moshe Chaim Luzzatto writes in *Path of the Just,* "One who possesses much wisdom is responsible to teach it to those who need it."[2]

But being told that this is what we must do isn't the whole of the story. There is a principle involved, as well. The Jewish approach to spiritual growth warns us not to fall prey to thinking that we could possibly pursue a spiritual life for ourselves without taking care of others along the way. By setting our intention to teach others, even as we pursue our own learning and growth, we are already thinking beyond ourselves and our own self-development. In the Jewish view, that's essential. Taking care of yourself and your own needs exclusive of others actually stunts your spiritual growth.

An analogy that captures this situation is the contrast between the Sea of Galilee and the Dead Sea. Both bodies of water are fed by the Jordan River, but while the Sea of Galilee is home to twenty types of fish and is surrounded by lush vegetation, the Dead Sea is every bit as lifeless as its name suggests. What's the difference? Water flows into the Sea of Galilee and then out again, whereas the Dead Sea has no outlet. Like that, one who learns but does not pass it on will be barren. In the words of the sages, who invoke a different metaphor, a scholar is compared to a flask of scented oil. When the container is covered, its scent does not spread. But uncovered, it lends its fragrant aroma all around. "This is the difference between a scholar who studies and one who also teaches," they said.[3]

But isn't teaching others a sacrifice that takes time and energy away from one's own personal study and practice? Many sources tell us that there is no contradiction between pursuing your own spiritual growth and teaching others. In fact, they want us to understand that teaching others is directly in the interest of our own spiritual development, because when we do that, we learn and grow in the process. We read in *Pirkei Avot* 4:6, "Rabbi Yishmael the son of Rabbi Yossi would say: 'One who learns Torah in order to teach is given the opportunity to learn and teach.'" This means that if you set yourself to teaching others, you will be granted all it takes to learn and also to teach. No sacrifice is required.

Midrash Shmuel goes even further on this topic, saying that one who learns in order to teach "will be taught from the heav-

ens and the gates of Torah will open before him." The Alter of
Novarodok, the great Mussar teacher Rabbi Yosef Yozel Hurwitz (1847–1919), explains how this process works in practice.[4]
Not only is it not a sacrifice to spend time and effort teaching
others, our efforts to teach others engage us in an unparalleled
process of growth ourselves. He brings the example of Rav Preida, who had a student who ordinarily needed to be taught a
lesson a daunting four hundred times before he grasped it.[5] One
day, the student was distracted and at the end of the four hun-
dredth repetition still had not understood. Rav Preida then
taught him the lesson an additional four hundred times. The
Alter asks rhetorically, "How could Rav Preida have sacrificed
so much time on such a pupil? How is it he gave no thought to
his own progress?" The very opposite is the case, he says: "Only
through his forbearance and complete commitment did he reach
such a high level of Divine service and improvement of his soul-
traits." Were it not for his efforts to teach, which brought him
face to face with challenges he had to struggle to overcome, Rav
Preida would not have developed into the person who has been
admired as the paragon of patience since his story was recorded
in the Talmud almost two thousand years ago.

The lesson is that we grow through our efforts to teach others. Our own learning gains a profound new dimension and
becomes more activated for ourselves. As well, anyone who has
taught knows that when we teach others, we better retain our
own learning. Preparing and then delivering a lesson forces us to
clarify what we have learned, and the material also gets more
firmly etched in memory. This may be the understanding that
underlies the Talmudic saying "I learned much from my teachers, more from my colleagues, but most of all from my students."[6] Rabbi Chanina, who uttered these words, knew from
experience that when we undertake to give to others, we receive

a gift ourselves. This is certainly my own experience and the experience of many teachers.

When the first opportunity to teach Mussar came to me, I asked my Mussar teacher, Rabbi Perr, what he thought about me taking up that invitation. I wouldn't have done it without his permission and validation that I was ready to offer something of what I had learned to others, if he thought I was. Without hesitation he answered, "Go ahead. You'll learn so much." When you teach what you have learned, you not only avoid the pitfall of selfish spiritual practice, you gain greater clarity and deeper understanding of everything that you have learned.

Not everyone is comfortable with the idea of teaching. Who am I to teach? I have so much still to learn myself. I've got so many issues to work out before I'll be ready to teach others. There is likely to be some truth to every one of these (and other) doubts that are likely to arise when we confront the possibility of teaching others, but there is nothing new in these concerns. Rabbi Bahya ibn Paquda published *Duties of the Heart* in 1070, and in the introduction to that book he confesses to very much the same doubts. "As soon as I began acting on my decision to write the book, it occurred to me that someone like me was not equipped to write it. I believed I was too dull-witted and incapable of expressing myself well enough. I was afraid of burdening myself with something that would only demonstrate my limitations and that I was overstepping my bounds."[7]

But he overcame those thoughts and feelings, saying, "I knew many good ideas were rejected because of fear, that dread causes a lot of damage, and I recalled the expression, 'Be careful not to be too careful.' I realized that if everyone who ever resolved to do something good or to instruct others in the path of righteousness kept still until he himself could accomplish everything he set out to, that nothing would have been said since the days of the prophets."

This voice coming from almost a thousand years ago is a model for us. No matter what your level of learning or development, there is surely someone out there who needs to hear exactly what it is you have to teach. It does not display a lack of humility to share with others the gifts you have received yourself.

PRACTICE

Ask yourself, What have I learned recently? Who could benefit from me sharing this lesson with them? How can I teach it to them?

Then look for a way to teach something you've learned to someone else.

Afterward, observe what effect teaching the other person had on you? Were you forced to clarify a concept? Did you have to learn something additional? Did you get a stronger impression of the subject because of the experience of sharing it with another person?

לומד על מנת לעשות

[45]

Learning in Order to Do

Lomed al menat la'Asot

More than you study, do.

—PIRKEI AVOT 6:5

THE LAST CHAPTER focused on the necessity of teaching others. Now we are being told that our own spiritual progress requires that we not only teach but also "do" ourselves. What path are we to follow to bring our learning into action in this way?

The study of Jewish sources can engage the mind just like the study of science or mathematics or art history. Intellectual accomplishments can be very satisfying, and brilliant scholars have always been stars in the Jewish world; but we are cautioned not to fall prey to thinking that cerebral learning is the goal of our spiritual activities. As students of Mussar, our goal is *shleimut*—wholeness or completeness—and *kedusha*, holiness. If we satisfy the mind and even impress others with our brilliance but don't engage in actions that reflect and embody what we have been learning, we move no closer to the wholeness and holiness we seek.

240

The Mussar teachers have been hardheaded in evaluating what does and does not work to bring about personal transformation, and their conclusion is that the mind is generally a weak tool for effecting spiritual growth. In the words of the Alter of Novarodok:[1]

But if one knows . . . only with his mind and not with his senses, he will find that his mental effort yields only a mental [i.e., intellectual] result, not a sensory [i.e., actual] one. As the Sages said, "The wicked know that their fate is evil and bitter, but it is too hard for them to change." Even though the mental effort enables him to quiet the ferment of human nature and evil attributes while he is speaking of moral ideals, he cannot at all master his predilections and forego his passions and rejoice in the verdict of God, because his effort was not to educate himself to put things into actual practice, but only to comprehend mentally the proper world-view, the whole way of life, the "how, what and when." . . .

At the moment of trial, he is like a blind person who never saw the light, because then the cloud covers the sun and he can see nothing. His whole exalted knowledge exists either before the fact or after the fact, but when the situation is at hand, the distraction of the trial makes him like a different person. Looking back he will say, "At the time of the trial, I was not the same person that I am now, after the trial."

These ideas reflect the general Mussar approach, which credits experience and not ideas alone with the power to transform. Of course, ideas are the starting point, because we need to form mental intentions and to identify the ideals we seek, but only when we enact those ideas in reality will the heart be touched and change brought about. It's with this exact process in mind that Rabbi Elya Lopian defined Mussar as "making the heart feel what the mind understands."[2]

Learning is just not enough if what you learn remains lodged between your ears, because if that is as far as the learning goes, it is not likely to have the strength to govern your actual behavior when "the cloud covers the sun and [you] can see nothing," as happens when emotions flare in real-life situations, obscuring the intellect. Real change requires that we activate our learning with doing.

There are two distinct ways to understand how to put "learning in order to do" into practice. The simplest to appreciate is that when a person combines study with actual practice, putting the concept studied directly into action, then that idea is bound to become engrained more deeply within his or her essence.

As an example we have a law taught in the Torah: "If you see your enemy's donkey lying under its burden would you refrain from helping him? You shall surely help along with him."[3] The Talmud expands and gives the rationale for this law: "If a friend requires help unloading, and an enemy loading, one's [first] obligation is toward his enemy in order to subdue his evil inclination [yetzer ha'ra]."[4] Helping your enemy is the priority, because that will bring you into encounter with your own inner spiritual adversary, which can only be vanquished through real-life encounters.

Well and good to know this, and quite another thing to do it. The text says "enemy," and that word falls so far short of capturing the explosive and hateful emotions we feel just seeing that person who has done us harm or undermined our just aspirations. In the face of the seething and powerful feelings, we are supposed to help him or her deal with a burden? Without learning, we would not have known that. Without doing it, we'd have no real experience of the effective spiritual stretch that is embedded in this law. By learning it, we know what is expected. By doing it, we encounter the transformative experience that renders us more whole.

The second idea is that when one studies with the intention of applying what one learns—even when that study is not accompanied by any concrete action—the study itself can be qualitatively different than when one studies without that intention. Activating the imagination with specific details and bringing the desire for change into the process of study can itself be a transformative process. This is a novel insight and one of the innovative concepts of the Mussar masters.

For example, *v'ahavta l'reacha kamocha*—"love your neighbor as yourself"[5]—is a sublime idea that is fundamental to Judaism. How can we "learn in order to do" that according to the second approach? The Mussar teachers tell us that just firming our intentions to implement the concept by envisioning the face of someone you intend to love and invoking the imagination to see that happening can have a real impact. Through strong intention and conjuring vivid mental images, modes of behavior will come alive, and we can count on being affected inwardly in the real way that is intended.

If your spiritual knowledge is theoretical and intellectual, you can't expect much good to come of it. When you put it into practice—whether in reality or in an exercise of imagination—you trigger experiences, and it is these that are the real agents of transformation. As the neurobiologists say, the neurons that fire together wire together. As we stimulate direct experience, so do we change the fundamental structure of our brains, and we become different people. Intellectual learning on its own does not have this potential.

Obviously, these two basic approaches are not mutually exclusive; they complement each other, and one should endeavor to practice both. The changes we will see may not be instantaneous, but they are assured. Slowly, over time, as Rav Yisrael promises, a new person will appear:[6]

> Let a person's heart not despair if he studies Mussar and is not awakened, or if he feels no impression on his soul motivating him to change his path. Through an abundance of [Mussar] study over an extended period of time, the impressions will accumulate, and he will be transformed into a different person.

PRACTICE

Rambam states that comforting mourners is a rabbinic commandment that fulfills the biblical injunction that we encountered in this discussion: "You shall love your neighbor as yourself."[7]

If you didn't know that before, you have now learned the biblical source for the requirement to give comfort to those who are bereaved.

To get the spiritual benefit of that *mitzvah* and to internalize its teaching, however, you have to do it. Do you know someone who is mourning a loss? Reach out to comfort that person *in deed*. Pick up the phone, send an e-mail, or better still, pay a visit to comfort the mourner.

המחכים את רבו

[46]

Making One's Teacher Wise

Ha'Machkim et Rabbo

As iron sharpens iron, so does one person sharpen another.

—PROVERBS 27:17

THIS METHOD of transformation literally translates as "one who *sharpens* his or her teacher." Traditionally, that "sharpness" has been understood to mean wisdom, which raises the question: What can a student do to make his or her teacher wiser?

One thing the student can do is ask sharp questions. Rabbi Chaim of Volozhin ruled that it is forbidden for a student to accept a teacher's words when he or she still has difficulties or questions.[1] No question should be ruled out because it is too basic, or foolish, or repetitive. The student is obligated to continue to ask, "I'm not clear on what this means" until it is explained satisfactorily. And the teacher (or parent, or supervisor, etc.) must try to explain again and again until the student understands. Like a blade being drawn repeatedly over a whetstone, each explanation not only clarifies for the student, it sharpens the teacher's wisdom.

"As iron sharpens iron, so does one person sharpen another."[2] Have you ever seen a chef sharpening a blade by scraping it against another knife? Or drawing a knife against a hardened steel rod? Honing iron against iron creates a sharp edge on the blade, just as the exchange of ideas among people sharpens their thinking.

Or to invoke a different metaphor, in the Talmud we read a teaching of Rabbi Nachman bar Yitzchak, who asked, "Why is Torah compared to a tree? As it is written, 'It is a Tree of Life for those who hold fast to it.' This is to teach that just as a small piece of wood can ignite a large one, so too do students of Torah sharpen their teachers."[3] And Rashi adds, "with their constant questioning."[4] Sometimes to answer the student's questions the teacher will need to do further research, and in this way, the student contributes to broadening the teacher's knowledge and wisdom.

These are all images meant to describe how alert, probing interactions not only generate facts but also serve to sharpen the minds of those involved. A number of Talmudic sages are said to have included in their lessons statements they knew were contrary to the law just to see whether the students were sufficiently on their toes to raise a challenge. Clearly, the student was expected and even encouraged to challenge the teacher, and it was understood that the teacher, as well as the student, would benefit from the challenge.[5]

We need this teaching, because this sort of behavior doesn't come easily to most of us. If we don't understand, we're shy to speak up. If the teacher goes too fast for us, we blame ourselves for not keeping up. If we think of a question, we might well dismiss it as too simplistic, likely to embarrass us for asking about something that everyone else probably understands. Here we are being told not to hold back, because we are not the only potential beneficiary of our questions. It is also a service to our teachers to ask our questions: They need our abrasion to become sharp.

Sometimes the student even catches out the teacher! Rav Yisrael Salanter would deliver a talk every week, and every week, students would ask him questions. During one such talk, just as Rav Yisrael was concluding a complicated discourse, someone challenged him with a question that destroyed his whole argument. Rav Yisrael paused only briefly, then admitted he was wrong and stepped down from the dais.

It takes a wise teacher to accept the kinds of questions from students that will increase his or her own wisdom. We find modeling for that accepting attitude in a famous story in the Talmud concerning the oven of Achnai.[6] The rabbis align in the argument such that Rabbi Eliezer is the sole opponent to consensus. He doesn't give up, however, and calls out, "If I am right, let the carob tree prove it by flying through the air." And it does. But the majority retorts, "We don't accept legal rulings from trees." Then Rabbi Eliezer says that if he is right, the stream should flow backwards, which it does. The rabbis also reject basing a legal decision on a stream. Then he orders the walls of the synagogue to collapse, and as they start to lean, Rabbi Yehoshua rebukes them, saying, "If sages argue with one another, what business do you have interfering?" So they don't collapse but remain leaning. Then Rabbi Eliezer appeals to heaven, and a divine voice replies, saying, "Why are you disputing with Rabbi Eliezar, for the law accords with him everywhere?" Rabbi Yehoshua then rises to his feet and says, "It is not in Heaven,"[7] meaning that rulings on law happen on earth, not in heaven, so even the heavenly voice has no standing in the rabbis' decisions. At that, the heavenly voice was heard to exclaim in delight, "My children have bested Me! My children have bested Me!"

God's response to the rabbis is a model for how a teacher should interact with students, and that model would apply equally to parent with child, supervisor with staff, and so forth. While we don't have any potential to "sharpen" God, we learn from this story that the teacher ought to delight in the student coming up with the right answer, and maybe even delivering a better answer than the teacher. A teacher's greatest joy ought to lie in being surpassed by those whom he or she has taught, then learning from those students.

Perhaps this idea lies at the heart of the directive we find in *Pirkei Avot* 1:6 to "Make for yourself a teacher." It's important that the teaching says "make" and not "find." It is not enough just to find someone who has the knowledge we seek and to attend that teacher's lectures. Rather, we have a role in *creating* the mentor we need by means of our own efforts to learn, including the questioning we do. We appoint that person to the status of being wiser than we are in the particular area we seek to learn. Then, by relentlessly questioning and seeking to wring answers from our teacher, we make him or her wiser still. Through these efforts we will have "created" that teacher.

Our efforts sharpen the abilities of the one who can teach us, and, in that way, we make that person into the teacher we need. The teacher, the other students, and we ourselves are all beneficiaries, and through that process, more of the wisdom in the world will be opened to us.

PRACTICE

Is there someone you can question to help clarify a situation? Bear in mind as you question that you are seeking to sharpen or make wiser the authority in that subject whom you are questioning.

המכוון את שמועתו

[47]

Clarifying What One Has Heard

Ha'Mechaven et shmu'ato

Let the wise one hear and increase learning. The understanding person shall acquire wise counsels.

—PROVERBS 1:5

W E ARE NEARING the end of these lessons on personal transformation, and it is wise advice to make a practice of clarifying what we have heard. That applies to these lessons but also to things we learn every day. Reality is complex, and it takes some determination to sort through the complexity to clarify for ourselves the essence of the lesson. That's the kernel we need to retain, which can be lost to us if we don't engage in this clarification process.

We may sit in a class nodding in agreement, or we may casually read something; but if we don't make the effort to understand the true intended message, we fool ourselves into thinking that we have learned something when really we haven't. Have you put in the time and effort necessary to truly understand the forty-six previous lessons, to uncover the foundation upon which each lesson was built? Have you made the effort to summarize the key points of each lesson in writing? Can you recall what you have been taught? Even just yesterday?

We are being urged to clarify the foundation of the lessons we hear and to try to understand their true intended meaning. To clarify the foundation means discerning the essence and the fundamental principle that is being conveyed. For example, if you were studying the rules of negative speech, you would encounter the law that prohibits speaking disparagingly about other people. But what about speaking negatively about inanimate objects, like your old car? What about a country? What's the practice there? Only by understanding the essence of the teaching can we understand how it applies, especially in situations that extend away from the most typical case.

Here is a brief glimpse of an answer, to illustrate the point. The *midrash* tells us that the section in the Torah about the spies follows the section that tells of Miriam, Moses's sister, being punished for speaking badly about Moses.[1] The *midrash* comments that the spies saw what happened to Miriam, and they did not take the lesson to heart—or, in the actual language of the text, they "did not take the Mussar." They went on to repeat the same behavior by speaking disparagingly about the land of Israel, and for that they were severely criticized.

In fairness, could we really expect the spies to have learned this lesson from what happened to Miriam? She spoke badly about a person, after all, while they spoke badly about a land, an inanimate object. The answer is that the same inner motivator that causes someone to speak badly about people can also show up in speech about inanimate objects. At root, it is the same issue and hence governed by the same approach. Delving deeply into whatever we learn is how we discover the fundamental principle that is being conveyed.

The bar is set for us in this area by Rabbi Elchanan Wasserman,[2] who used to travel to spend Rosh Hashana and Yom Kippur with his teacher, the Chafetz Chaim. One year, after the Chafetz Chaim spoke, someone commented that he had given the very same talk the previous year. Rav Elchanan told the person that he was mistaken because the Chafetz Chaim had, in fact, used several different words the previous year.

Imagine being so exacting and deep in your listening and learning. Yet that level is not really so beyond us as it may seem. If you were being trained to fly an airplane or do surgery, no one would expect you to hear a lesson once and then be ready to jump behind the controls or pick up a scalpel. In those situations, there is clearly too much at stake to depend on a single run-through of a lesson. You'd review as much as possible and expect to be thoroughly drilled and tested before you got anywhere near a real application of what you had learned.

It's amazing, then, to think how casual we can be with our own lives and souls. Is your life not precious to you? Aren't the stakes very high when you consider how deeply the decisions you make affect your own well-being and the welfare of those around you, in this life, for sure, and maybe for all eternity?

The more we understand what we learn, the more it connects with our inner essence and becomes part of who we are—the more of it we will retain as an enduring feature of ourselves. If you take the time and make the effort to assimilate your lessons, discern the fundamental principle, delve deeply into understanding the reasoning, take up a notebook (or keyboard) and summarize the ideas, that will help you to absorb the message into the very fabric of your being. This is what it takes to acquire wisdom.

Rabbi Shlomo Wolbe made a version of this practice the cornerstone of his Mussar instruction. No matter what subject he was teaching, he always encouraged his students to look deeply into matters to see what they could learn from their own experiences—*hitlamdut* he called that, which can be translated as "self-instruction" or "teaching yourself," and the clear implication is "from your own experience." *Hitlamdut* is how we clarify and internalize what lies at the core of whatever it is we are learning.

Rabbi Wolbe himself wrote about this form of deeper learning: "This is not a single character trait, but a signpost for life of someone who works at Mussar. And if we only did it for this, it would have been enough: if all the Mussar work were to bring us to this self-instruction alone, this would already be a great goal."[3]

This practice applies to lessons learned from a teacher, as well as to lessons learned from life experience. In both cases, it is up to us to extract the clear essence from the complexity of the original. When we take that step to clarify, we are not just hearing the lesson, we are teaching it to ourselves. This is how the heart changes.

To return to our example of hurtful speech, it is taught that gossip kills three people: the one who speaks it, the one who listens, and the one about whom it is spoken.[4] And in your life experience, you are likely to have seen and felt the pain brought on by gossip, because gossip is so prevalent. But have you clarified for yourself the very essence of the prohibition on gossip, and have you taught that lesson to yourself in such a way as to embed it in your heart, to become a part of your human essence? That additional step makes all the difference.

The lessons are there. Do you hear them? And if you do, are they clear to you? Do you want to take them to heart? Then approach learning and growing as requiring that you be conscious about what you take away from the lesson.

We are near the end. It is very important to recognize that whenever you learn something, you should build a process of review and clarification into your plan.

PRACTICE

What did you just learn? Review the lesson and then come up with your own language that synthesizes and captures the essence of this practice, as it is meaningful to you.

Write out your own brief note. You are sure to find that by the time you have completed that brief review and written out the few words that describe this practice, you will know it more thoroughly and deeply than you did when you first read the lesson. That, in itself, is the meta-lesson.

האומר דבר בשם אומרו

[48]

Saying Something in the Name of Its Speaker

Ha'Omer Davar be'Shem Omro

Whoever repeats a statement in the name of the one who said it brings redemption to the world.

—CHULLIN 104B

OUR FINAL METHOD of acquiring Torah is surprising. The grand climax is a directive to give credit to anyone from whom we have learned something. The importance of quoting sources is learned from the story of Esther. When Mordechai told her about a plot to assassinate the king, she informed the king in the name of Mordechai. Later, the whole story turns on the king remembering the great service done to him by Mordechai, as he had learned because Queen Esther had quoted her source.

There are several reasons to give credit to the person from whom you learned something. The Purim story provides a good example, and based on that story the Talmud teaches that quoting in the name of another brings redemption.[1] Had Esther not mentioned Mordechai's name when she passed along the information about the plot against the king's life, events might have taken a different and disastrous turn. Because she did mention Mordechai, the Jews were saved. This tells us that there can be much more at stake to justify citing your sources than just courtesy or good manners.

At a more mundane level, when you acknowledge that your ideas have roots, you let others know who and what has influenced your thinking. This gives context and depth to your ideas and situates you in a line of people whose thinking you appreciate. Others will understand you much better when you provide this contextualizing information along with the ideas.

By citing the name of the person who taught you something, you also honor your teachers. Rabbi Elazar ben Shamua said, "The reverence you show your teacher should be like the reverence you hold for heaven,"[2] and quoting your teacher's name is surely an act of respect.

At the most elementary level, when you cite your source, you are honoring truth. It is simply true that the idea came from this one or that one and not yourself. The importance of adhering to truth in that way is underlined by Rabbeinu Yonah, who tells us, "We have been commanded to limit ourselves to the truth, because it is one of the foundations of the soul."[3] If you repeat an idea you derived from someone else without citing that source, you give the impression that the idea originated with you and thus propagate a falsehood, weakening the foundation of your own soul.

One who is always careful to give credit where it is due also displays humility, because he or she is saying that what I have is no cause for pride because this idea derives from others. That recognition opens a person to more learning, unimpeded by ego.

In contrast, the Torah castigates one who proclaims, "My

strength and the might of my hand made me all this wealth."[4] To make clear that there is no logic to taking personal credit for gifts we have received, the Torah continues, "Then you should remember HaShem, your God, that it was God who gave you the strength to make wealth."[5]

Indeed, if we can have the humility to recognize that there is a single Source to every blessing that we receive in every area of our lives and we give thanks to God, we will actually be fulfilling our directive to "say something in the name of its speaker."[6]

The Talmud tells us,[7] "Rav Yitzchak said: 'If one says, I labored [in the study of Torah] but did not succeed,'[8] do not believe him. If he says, 'I have not labored [in the study of Torah], yet I have succeeded,' do not believe him. If he says, 'I have labored [in the study of Torah] and I have succeeded,' believe him." The Vilna Gaon asks why the term *metziah*—to find or not find it (as in finding a lost object)—is used here as a way of saying that one has succeeded or not succeeded in one's studies. The answer is that when we find something, it is not based on our own effort—we just come upon it. Even after we have put in much toil and effort to study Torah and practice spirituality, in the final analysis, whatever comes to us remains something we "find," something we receive as a gift from God.

Rabbi Moshe Chaim Luzzatto cites this very concept in the words with which he begins the final chapter of *Path of the Just,* on the subject of holiness: "Holiness is two-fold. Its beginning is labor and its end reward; its beginning, exertion and its end, a gift."[9]

What does tradition say about someone who does not acknowledge the name of the one from whom they learned something? Failing to give credit to sources is tantamount to stealing.[10] More specifically, that person is guilty of *genevat da'at*—literally, "stealing a mind," which refers to words or actions that could cause others to form incorrect conclusions. Our rabbis teach, "There are seven types of thieves, and the first among them is one who steals the minds of others."[11] Not quoting the source of one's ideas can be a violation of the prohibition on "stealing minds."

And we had better be accurate. Another source warns, "One who says something in the name of someone who didn't say it brings a curse upon the world."[12]

The strongest argument for quoting sources is that the one who quotes situates himself or herself in the chain of a tradition. The modern world celebrates innovation and uniqueness, and that minimizes the wisdom of tradition that provides us with time-tested templates for wise living. Human nature has not changed in the last few thousand years, and neither have the pitfalls and hazards that come with living a human life. Referencing what we learn from those who came before us is not obsessive acknowledgment of intellectual property rights; it is a demonstration to others and a reminder to ourselves that we came from somewhere, that we have learned from those who came before us, and that we are indebted to them for the legacy of wisdom and guidance they bequeathed to us.

So it is fitting that we close this last lesson by acknowledging the guidance we have received through this study and practice from *Pirkei Avot* 6:6. The first five chapters of *Pirkei Avot* focus on guidelines for good, honest, ethical human living. The sixth, which was added later, is different, in that it focuses on the Torah and the spiritual rewards that come to those who study it. We don't know who wrote the section of *Pirkei Avot* that has been our guide in this book, and so the best we can do is to acknowledge all the sages of the Mishnaic period who transmitted an oral tradition from teacher to student until it came to be written down and codified in the Mishnah. The teachings of the oral

WITH HEART IN MIND

tradition passed through many minds in the process of transmission and so represent a collective effort.

In acknowledging the source of our learning, we bow in gratitude to a wise tradition that has been bequeathed to us, that we might live better, purer, holier lives, for our own sake, for the sake of those around us, and for the sake of those who will come after us.

PRACTICE

The ideas you speak will likely have been learned from someone. Make a special effort to give credit to the one who taught you what you have spoken.

Conclusion: *With Heart in Mind*

The world is rich in potential, as are we who live within it. We are endowed with astounding gifts like the ability to think, speak, be logical, cooperate, care. And since we have free will, it is entirely in our hands to decide how to put our many gifts of heart and mind to work.

The Mussar teachers are perfectly clear in identifying that the primary aspect of a human being is the spiritual essence that lies within. Our bodily makeup is determined by our DNA, which overlaps closely with that of chimpanzees. Our emotions and desires are really not much different from those of dogs and cats. Many animals have intelligence and some even have rudimentary forms of speech. The primary thing that sets us apart is our spiritual nature, and fulfilling our uniquely human destiny involves realizing the potential of the soul. "A person's primary mission in the world is to purify and elevate the soul," is how the Mussar teacher Rabbi Yechezkiel Levenstein put it.[1]

Some people dedicate their lives to their bodies, whether perfecting them in the gym or on the sports field or indulging their senses. Others live in a world of the mind, stressing the intellect. For still others, it may be the pursuit of beauty or expression. There are people who pour themselves into community service, social action, politics. Some orient their lives to accumulating wealth and possessions. It is so clear that we can spend the gifts of our lives almost any way we choose. Yet committing all of who we are and what we have to our soul-life is the most uniquely human way to live. It makes the most of our potential, because, from a Jewish perspective, it involves all of ourselves—body, mind, emotions, desires, aesthetics, community, and so on.

The Jewish view is that holiness is the highest human possibility to which we can aspire. The Torah gives us that guideline in no uncertain terms: "You shall be holy," it says in several places and several ways. There is no aspect of the world that does not have the potential to be holy; it all depends on how that aspect is used. And there is no part of ourselves that can be neglected in seeking holiness, as if we could claim to have cleaned our garden when we had only uprooted half of the weeds. In no time they would be everywhere again.

The founder of the Novarodok school of Mussar, Rabbi Yosef Yozel Hurwitz, offers a clear analogy to dispel the illusion that a person could be pure in the house of worship and crooked in the marketplace, for example. He says that's like trying to purify your kitchen one utensil at a time. No sooner would something be cleansed than it would be defiled again by contact with the unwashed things around it.

The pursuit of holiness calls on us, not to withdraw from the material and worldly dimensions of life, but rather to apply the desires of the body in holy ways, use our possessions honestly and fairly, express our creativity in ways that don't harm or demean others, engage the intellect in things that have a valuable impact on self and other, and so on. That's the path we have been exploring in this book—there are so many chapters because our lives have many dimensions, and each requires its own guidance.

The pathway we have been following doesn't lead up to a cave in the mountains or to a hut in the desert but clears the way to holiness right within the world of business, the life of the mind, our sense of humor, our egos, our desires, our aspirations, and all the other topics we have covered. Those are our gifts; we have been learning how to use them well in the light of thousands of years of Jewish experience. There is no place to seek holiness other than where you are right now.

If I am to be precise, however, the original source that inspired this book and that provided all the methods we have explored doesn't speak of holiness. It speaks of acquiring Torah. What's the connection between holiness and the steps to personal transformation we have explored in the name of acquiring Torah?

The methods of personal practice opened up for you in this book mark out the way toward holiness. We have been focusing on the path, because the goal is a given. Judaism draws its wisdom for living from the Torah, and the Torah couldn't be clearer in highlighting and underlining that holiness is the beacon toward which we should orient our lives.

The holiness that the Torah directs us to seek won't be found in a pot at the end of the rainbow but is a hidden treasure buried within each of us. When you walk the pathway laid out in this book, it doesn't provide you holiness, it removes the obstacles to the holiness that is already and inherently abundant within you. Too much engagement in business is an obstacle. Being egotistical is an obstacle. Excessive or quick anger is an obstacle. Judging others negatively is an obstacle. Whether stated in the positive or the negative, every method explored here has as its purpose to remove a barrier that obstructs the light of holiness that glows within you from shining into your life and through you into the world.

Not every method in this book applies to you, because not everyone has all the same obstacles to holiness. Some will be intensely relevant, others moderately so, some little at all. Knowing yourself and what stands in the way of your own purification and elevation is essential, as that will guide you to give special focus to practicing the transformative methods that your life needs more than others. That's how you use your mind to develop your heart.

The commandments found in the Torah are the obligations of the religious life, and we have to wonder why it might be that the main lists of commandments do not include "You shall be holy." It sounds a lot like a commandment, but in fact it isn't. Again, the Alter of Novarodok, Rabbi Yosef Yozel Hurwitz, offers us an insight: Sometimes things that are stated like commandments actually are not that; they are really just good advice.[2]

In the case of holiness, the directive to pursue that goal is best understood as good advice, because unlike a commandment, advice leaves the choice in our hands. No one can really convince you to make holiness your goal. No one can make you do the practices in this book. You have to want to. You have to hear a call from deep within that is reverberating with these words. Only your own motivation will propel you along on the journey.

There's no hitchhiking on the spiritual path. There are no shortcuts to holiness. It's a stairway to heaven, not an elevator. The methods we have drawn upon were pointed out for us 2,000 years ago. I've done my best to lay them out clearly in the preceding chapters. Only you can take the next step.

Notes

INTRODUCTION

1. *Rosh Hashanah* 21.
2. *Hilchot Teshuvah* (*Laws of Repentance*) 5:2.
3. In the Talmud (*Kiddushin* 32b), the sage Rava cites Psalms 1:2, which says, "And in his Torah he meditates day and night," in support of the idea that one is meant to "acquire" the wisdom of Torah, to make it "his Torah"—i.e., part and parcel of one's being.
4. Born in Poland in 1872, died in Israel in 1970.
5. *Bridging the Gap* (Jerusalem and New York: Feldheim, 2007), p. 148.
6. Rabbi Elijah ben Shlomo Zalman Kremer (1720–97).
7. Known as the Alter of Kelm (1824–98).

CHAPTER 1. *Study*

1. *Chagigah* 5b.
2. Deuteronomy 11:19.

3. *Shir HaShirim Rabbah* 8.
4. *Nefesh ha'Chaim*, gate 4, chapter 10.
5. Rabbi Avraham Yeshaya Karelitz (1878–1953); *Kovetz Igrot* 1:1.
6. From his book *Chochma U'Mussar* (New York: Yerucham Levovitz, 1957), vol. 2, chapter 113.
7. On Proverbs 19:9 and in his commentary to *Berachot* 8a.
8. "May My teaching drop like rain, may My utterance flow like dew" (Deuteronomy 32:2).

CHAPTER 2. *Attentive Listening*

1. Published as *Ohr Yisrael* (*The Light of Israel*), in 1890, originally in Hebrew and now also available in an English translation by Rabbi Zvi Miller (Southfield, Mich.: Targum Press, 2004).
2. Deuteronomy 6:4.
3. Jeremiah 6:10.
4. See the Vilna Gaon's commentary to Proverbs 11:2 for more on the connection between humility and learning.
5. As quoted in Fertig, *Bridging the Gap*, p. 37.

CHAPTER 3. *Orderly Speech*

1. In about 110 C.E.
2. Genesis 2:7.
3. *Ruach memalala.*
4. *Nefesh HaChaim* 1:15.
5. *Orot HaKodesh,* vol. 3, p. 285.
6. Genesis 1:3.
7. "With ten utterances the world was created" (*Pirkei Avot* 5:1).
8. Commentary to *Pirkei Avot* 1:17.

9. *Arachin* 15b.
10. Rabbi Yisrael Meir HaKohen Kagan wrote two major works on the laws of speech: *Chafetz Chaim* (*Desirer of Life*) and *Shmirat HaLashon* (*Guarding the Tongue*), both 1873.
11. *Chofetz Chaim: A Lesson a Day* (Brooklyn, N.Y.: Mesorah Publications, 1995), p. 53.

CHAPTER 4. *Understanding of the Heart*

1. In some versions, this method is given as *kavanat ha'lev,* the intentions of the heart. Some versions of *Pirkei Avot* have this method as *sichlut halev,* which literally is "intelligence of the heart."
2. *Kohelet Rabbah* 1:36.
3. 1 Kings 3:5.
4. "Solomon's wisdom was greater than the wisdom of all the people of the East, and greater than all the wisdom of Egypt" (1 Kings 4:30).
5. *Da'at Torah* (Jerusalem: Daas Torah Publications, 1976, 1995), vol. 2, p. 102.
6. There is a history of such divine agents assisting Jewish teachers, including Rabbi Yosef Karo and Rabbi Moshe Chaim Luzzatto. Such an emissary is known as a *maggid.* This story is from Rabbi Chaim of Volozhin's introduction to the Vilna Gaon's *Safra d'Tzniuta.*
7. *Iggeret HaGra,* included with his work *Even Shleimah,* edited by Rabbi Shmuel of Slotzk (Vilna, Lithuania: Tzvi Hirsch, 1924).

CHAPTER 5. *Fear*

1. Exodus 24:12–18.
2. *Shabbat* 87b–88a.

3. "Iggeret Ha'Mussar" (The Mussar Letter), in *Ohr Yisrael,* trans. Zvi Miller (Southfield, Mich.: Targum Press, 2004), pp. 391–409.
4. Ibid., p. 397.
5. A *yirei shamayim.*
6. *Path of the Just,* trans. Shraga Silverstein (Jerusalem and New York: Feldheim, 1966), chapter 24, p. 313.
7. Exodus 20:17.
8. *Berachot* 33b.
9. *Ein Eyah* (Jerusalem: Machon Hartzyah, 1995), vol. 3, p. 157.
10. Ibid.

CHAPTER 6. *Awe*

1. *Berachot* 28b.
2. *Orot Ha'Kodesh* (Lights of Holiness; Jerusalem: Mossad Ha'Rav Kook, 1963), 1:83.
3. Jonah 1:16.
4. "The *yirah* of the Lord is the beginning of wisdom: and the knowledge of the holy is understanding" (Proverbs 9:10).
5. *Da'at Chochma U'Mussar,* vol. 2, chapters 51–53 (Brooklyn, N.Y.: Da'as Chochmah U'Mussar Publications, 1972).

CHAPTER 7. *Humility*

1. Referring here to *anavah,* the most common, though not the only, term for "humility" in Hebrew.
2. Numbers 12:13.
3. Exodus 2:11.
4. Exodus 2:13.
5. Exodus 2:17.

6. Known as Rebbi, or "our holy teacher," b. 135 C.E. The Mishnah is an authoritative collection of interpretive material embodying the oral tradition of Jewish law and forming the first part of the Talmud, compiled about 200 C.E.
7. *Sotah* 49a.
8. Known as the Netziv.
9. *Sanhedrin* 42a, citing Proverbs 14:4.
10. *Path of the Just,* chapter 22.
11. In the Talmud, *Avodah Zarah* 20b, referring to Isaiah 61:1.
12. *Chochma U'Mussar,* vol. 2, *ma'amar* 115, p. 95.

CHAPTER 8. *Joy*

1. 1 Samuel 18:1.
2. The sages referred to Abraham, Isaac, and Jacob as *yesharim,* as in *Avodah Zarah* 25a.
3. Psalms 119:14.
4. *Yishrei lev.*
5. *Pirkei Avot* 2:4.
6. Leviticus 19:1.
7. שמח and צמח.

CHAPTER 9. *Serving the Sages*

1. 2 Kings 3:11.
2. *Berachot* 7b.
3. *Bamidbar Rabbah* 21:14.
4. *Sotah* 22a, *Berachot* 47b; "ignoramus" is *am ha'aretz.*
5. Rabbi Simcha Zissel Ziv (1824–98) was a primary disciple of Rav Yisrael Salanter and the founder and director of the Kelm Yeshiva. He was known as the "Alter of Kelm," *alter* meaning "elder," an appellation of honor.

6. Based on volume 2 of *Tenuat HaMussar* (The Mussar Movement), by Rabbi Dov Katz (Tel Aviv: Bitan haSefer Publishing, 1952, 1963).

CHAPTER 10. *Closeness to Friends*

1. *Ta'anit* 23a; *ha'ma'agal* means "the circle maker."
2. It sounds better in Aramaic: "*O chevrusa o mesusa.*"
3. Lectures he gave in the years between the Six-Day War and the Yom Kippur War were collected and published as "*Psychiatria ve'Dat*" ("Psychiatry and Religion") in the journal *Bishvilei ha'Refu'ah*, vol. 5, Sivan 5742, pp. 57–90.
4. *Ta'anit* 7a.
5. *Kiddushin* 30b.
6. Ibid.
7. *Chochma U'Mussar* (New York: Ateret Roshanu, 2000), vol. 2, p. 284; *ma'amar* 290.
8. *Strive for Truth!,* edited by Rabbi Aryeh Carmell (New York: Feldheim, 1978), vol. 1, p. 130.
9. *Sukkah* 52b.
10. Founder of the Sassov Chassidic dynasty.

CHAPTER 11. *Debating with Students*

1. Genesis 18:16–33.
2. *Sanhedrin* 111b.
3. *Shabbat* 31a.
4. *Kiddushin* 30b.
5. *Ohr Yisrael*, letter 6.
6. *Pirkei Avot* 5:17.
7. *Ta'anit* 7a.
8. *Derech Chayim* (a commentary on *Pirkei Avot;* Jerusalem: Makhon Yerushalayim, 2005).

9. *Ta'anit* 7a.
10. *Baba Metzia* 84a.
11. Rabbi Shmuel Eliezer Edels (1555–1631).
12. *Sanhedrin* 42b.

CHAPTER 12. *Settledness*

1. *Eruvin* 65a.
2. Rabbeinu Nissim of Catalonia in the tenth essay in his work *Derashot HaRan* (Jerusalem: Beit Ha'Mussar, 1986).
3. *Alei Shur*, vol. 1, pp. 194–96.
4. *Michtav mi'Eliyahu*, vol. 4 (Tel Aviv: Sifriati Religious Book Agency, 2001), p. 240.
5. *Ein Ayah,* part 2 (Jerusalem: Makhon Rabbi Tzvi Yehudah Kook, 1987), 111.

CHAPTER 13. *Studying the Written and Oral Torah*

1. *Kiddushin* 30a.
2. Deuteronomy 6:8.
3. In regard to *tefillin,* the Talmud fills in many details. See *Menachot* 34–37.
4. *Megillah* 16b.
5. *Mishnah Pe'ah* 1:1.

CHAPTER 14. *Purity*

1. For example, in Leviticus 14:8, where a person defiled by disease is given instructions to wash and be cleansed.
2. Post-Talmudic writers of rabbinic glosses on Biblical and Talmudic texts.
3. *Path of the Just,* trans. Shraga Silverstein (Jerusalem and New York: Feldheim, 1966), p. 205.
4. "Rabbi Elazar ha'Kappar said: 'Envy, lust and the pursuit

of honor take a person out of this world'" (*Pirkei Avot* 4:21), again bringing out the theme of separation.

5. *Path of the Just,* chapter 16.
6. *Shabbat* 119b.
7. Reish Lakish.

CHAPTER 15. *Limiting Sleep*

1. *Hilchot Deot* 3, 3.
2. *Pirkei Avot* 3:4–5.
3. Introduction to the *Biur HaGra,* the commentary the Vilna Gaon wrote on the *Shulchan Aruch.*
4. This practice is referred to as *tikkun chatzot*—literally, the fixing (in a spiritual sense) at midnight. While this custom is not widely practiced today, even among the most pious Jews, it is mentioned in the first chapter of the *Shulchan Aruch,* the code of Jewish law, not as a directive but as something that was practiced.
5. Joshua 1:8 (emphasis is mine).
6. *Eruvin* 65a.
7. *Nedarim* 15a; also, Rav Yehudah: "Night was made for sleeping" (*Eruvin* 65).
8. *Path of the Just,* chapter 6.
9. *Hilchot Teshuvah* 3:4.

CHAPTER 16. *Limiting Conversation*

1. Deuteronomy 6:7.
2. Reported in Rabbi Chaim Ephraim Zaitchik, *Sparks of Mussar* (New York: Feldheim, 1985), p. 31.
3. Literally, "fence"; *Pirkei Avot* 3:17.
4. *Derech Chayim,* commentary on *Pirkei Avot* 1:17.
5. *Orot Ha'Kodesh* 3:273.

6. *Pirkei Avot* 1:17.
7. 1914–2005; spoken to his Mussar group (*va'ad*) on 16 Iyar 5761 (May 9, 2001).
8. *Hilchot Deot* 2:4.

CHAPTER 17. *Limiting Work or Business*

1. *Sparks of Mussar*, p. 223.
2. *Avot D'Rabbi Natan* 11:1.
3. *Kohelet Rabbah* 9:9.
4. See the Ramban's commentary to Leviticus 19:1.
5. *Hilchot Talmud Torah* 3:7.
6. *Berachot* 35b.

CHAPTER 18. *Limiting Levity*

1. *Pesachim* 117a; *Shabbat* 30b.
2. *Ta'anit* 22a.
3. *Sotah* 42a.
4. *Path of the Just*, chapter 5.
5. The *akedah*; Genesis 22:1–19.
6. He is given the name in Genesis 22:3, and in verse 6, Sarah says, "God has made laughter for me; every one that hears will laugh on account of me."

CHAPTER 19. *Limiting Pleasure*

1. *Kiddushin* 4:12.
2. Rabbi Judah Loew, the Maharal of Prague (1525–1609), a seminal Jewish thinker in the post-medieval period.
3. *Sanhedrin* 111a.
4. *Da'at Torah*, vol. 1 (Jerusalem: Da'as Torah Publications, 1985), pp. 279–82.

5. The Chassidic school of Slonim is one of the only ones that makes Mussar an integral part of its method.
6. Genesis 28:12: "And behold a ladder standing on the earth, its head reaching up to heaven, and behold angels of God ascending and descending it."
7. Berezovsky, Shalom Noach (the Slonimer Rebbe), introduction to "Holiness," in *Netivot Shalom* (Jerusalem: Yeshivat Beit Avraham, 1994).
8. Ibid., "Holiness," section 7, chapter 2.
9. *Path of the Just,* chapter 1.
10. Jeremiah 2:13.
11. *Da'as Shlomo Geulah* (Jerusalem: Bais Ha'Mussar Publishing, 2010), p. 207.

CHAPTER 20. *Limiting Mundane Activities*

1. *Vayikra Rabbah,* chapter 9.
2. Rabbi Nosson Tzvi Finkel (1849–1927).
3. *Gadlus ha'adam.*
4. *Avot D'Rabbi Natan* 28.
5. *Ner HaShem nishmat adam*—"the human soul is the candle of God" (Proverbs 20:27).
6. *Ovdei HaShem.*
7. Deuteronomy 34:5.

CHAPTER 21. *Slow to Anger*

1. Exodus 34:6.
2. Moshe Miller, trans., *Palm Tree of Deborah,* (New York: Targum, 1993), chapter 1, section 1.
3. *Y'halachta b'd'rachav* (Deuteronomy 28:9).
4. Chabakuk 3:2.
5. Ecclesiastes 7:9.
6. *Pesachim* 66b.

7. See Proverbs 14:29 for a verse that echoes this idea.
8. *Shabbat* 105b.
9. The story appears in *Berachot* 18b and Rabbi Salanter's commentary in *Ohr Yisrael,* letter 26.

CHAPTER 22. *Goodheartedness*

1. Rabbi Yosef Rosen (1858–1936).
2. For example, *Pirkei Moshe* of HaRav Moshe Almosheninu (c.1515–c.1580), a distinguished rabbi who was born at Thessaloniki and died in Constantinople.
3. A German rabbi whose thought has been very influential in guiding the response of Orthodox Judaism to the modern world.
4. In his commentary to *Pirkei Avot* titled *Chapters of the Fathers* (Jerusalem and New York: Samson Rafael Hirsch Publication Society, 1967), p. 106.
5. In Tiferet Yisrael's commentary to *Pirkei Avot* 2:9.
6. *Sanhedrin* 106b.
7. Eliezer Papo, "Heart," in *Pele Yoetz* (New York: Sepher-Hermon Press, 1991).
8. *Avot D'Rabbi Natan* 13.
9. *Yoreh Deah* 249:3.
10. *"Tocho k'varo"* (*Berachot* 28a).
11. Exodus 4:14.
12. As explained by Rabbi Eliyahu Dessler, *Michtav M'Eliyahu,* vol. 4.
13. A Lithuanian contemporary and colleague of Rabbi Yisrael Salanter with whom he collaborated in fighting the harsh decrees of the Russian government.
14. *Even Shleimah,* chapter 1, *siman* (section) 11.
15. *Pirkei Avot* 2:13.

CHAPTER 23. *Faith in the Sages*

1. Known as *Chazal* (i.e., *Chachamenu zichronam liv'racha*—literally, "Our Sages, may their memory be blessed").
2. Deuteronomy 17:11.
3. Rabbi Shlomo Yitzhaki was a medieval French rabbi and author of comprehensive commentaries on the Talmud and written Torah.
4. *Michtav mi'Eliyahu*, vol. 4, p. 269.
5. Rabbi Akiva Eiger was a nineteenth-century Hungarian rabbi famous for his complex commentaries on the Talmud and works of Jewish law.
6. Rabbi Avraham Yeshaiya Karelitz (1878–1953).
7. The decline of the generations is a traditional rabbinic concept that says that every generatrion since the revelation at Mount Sinai has been weaker and less authoritative than the generations that preceded it.

CHAPTER 24. *Accepting Suffering*

1. *Pesachim* 115b.
2. Leviticus 10:1–3.
3. *Arachin* 16a.

CHAPTER 25. *Knowing One's Place*

1. As in *Pirkei Avot* 11:14, for example.
2. *Tiferet Yisrael* (Or EtZion: Merkaz Shapira, 2010).
3. See *Berachot* 31a and Tosafot there.
4. *Berachot* 31a.

CHAPTER 26. *Happiness with Your Portion*

1. *Berachot* 59b.
2. Respectfully, in the third person.

3. *Yoma* 38b; see the complete statement of Ben Azzai at the bottom of 38a–b.

CHAPTER 27. *Making a Fence around Your Activities*

1. See Exodus 23:13 and Leviticus 18:30.
2. *Sha'arei Teshuvah* 3:7.
3. *Da'at Torah,* vol. 3, p. 172.
4. *Kiddushin* 81a.
5. Jewish law permits a man to take a captive woman to himself but only after giving her a month to mourn the loss of her native family (Deuteronomy 21:10–15).

CHAPTER 28. *Not Claiming Credit for Oneself*

1. *Da'at Torah U'Mussar,* Shemot, p. 209.
2. *Sanhedrin* 88b.
3. *Path of the Just,* chapter 22.
4. Deuteronomy 8:17.
5. *Sanhedrin* 99b.

CHAPTER 29. *Being Beloved*

1. *Reishit Chochmah* (The Beginning of Wisdom: The Gate of Love), trans. Simcha Benyosef (Jersey City, N.J.: Ktav Publishing, 2002), p. 20.
2. 1 Samuel 18:1, 3.
3. *Sotah* 2a.
4. Proverbs 27:19.
5. *Berachot* 17a.
6. *Strive for Truth,* vol. 1, p. 19ff.
7. *K'ish echad, b'lev echad.* From Rashi's commentary to Exodus 19:2.
8. *Pirkei Avot* 3:10.

CHAPTER 30. *Loving God*

1. *Hilchot Teshuvah* 10:6.
2. *Hilkhot Yesodei Ha'Torah,* 2:1–2.
3. Psalms 19:2.

CHAPTER 31. *Loving God's Creatures*

1. *Musar Avichah,* Ahavah II (Jerusalem: Mossad Ha'Rav Kook, 1985).
2. Yehudah Loew (The Maharal), *Netivot Olam,* Ahavat haRe'i 1, trans. and adapted by Eliakim Willner (Brooklyn, N.Y.: Mesorah Publications, 1994).
3. *Horeb,* trans. I. Grunfeld (London: Soncino Press, 1962), chapter 17.
4. *Yerushalmi Nedarim* 9:4.
5. *Musar Avichah,* Ahavah II.
6. *Pirkei Avot* 1:12.
7. *Avot D'Rabbi Natan* 12.
8. No metaphor here. The text actually says that they kissed.
9. In the Talmud (*Yevamot* 65b) Rabbi Ila'i said that one is permitted to alter the truth for the sake of peace. Rabbi Nosson said doing so is actually a *mitzvah.* These teachings do not represent an abandonment of the principle of truthfulness but recognize that there are circumstances in which truth is subservient to a higher goal.
10. *"Tocho k'varo"* (*Berachot* 28a).

CHAPTER 32. *Loving Rebukes*

1. *Sha'arei Teshuvah* 2:12.
2. Leviticus 19:17.
3. *Aruchin* 16b.

4. Then a young student but destined to be the founder and rosh yeshiva of Yeshivat Chevron.
5. *Adam B'Yikar,* p. 25.
6. The nickname of Rabbi Yitzchok Blazer (1837–1907).
7. *Ohr Yisrael,* end of letter 20.
8. See Exodus 18:14–27.
9. *Tamid* 28a.

CHAPTER 33. *Love of Uprightness*

1. *Sichos Mussar* (Brooklyn, N.Y.: Mesorah Publications/ ArtScroll, 1989), p. 169.
2. *Sotah* 42a.
3. See Rabbeinu Yonah (*Sha'arei Teshuvah* 3:172–231) for details on each of these classes of people.
4. 1860–1939; rosh yeshiva in Grodno, Lithuania.
5. *Sha'arei Yosher,* as translated by Rabbi Micha Berger.

CHAPTER 34. *Distancing from Honor*

1. Known for his work *Sha'arei Tevunah* (Gates of Discernment; Piotrokow, Poland: H. Polman, 1925).
2. Esther 5:9–11.
3. Esther 5:13.
4. *Yevamot* 62b.
5. *Pirkei Avot* 4:1.
6. Michael Rosen, *The Quest for Authenticity: The Thought of Reb Simhah Bunim* (Jerusalem: Urim Publications, 2008), p. 124.
7. *Sotah* 49b.
8. In the words of the sages, "*zocheh l'shtei shulchanot*"—he merited to "be at two tables."
9. *Sha'arei Kedushah* (Gates of Holiness).
10. *Kiddushin* 32b.

CHAPTER 35. *Not Being Overly Satisfied in One's Learning*

1. *Ta'anit* 20a–b.
2. *Path of the Just,* chapter 22.
3. *Shaar Hak'niah,* chapter 9.
4. *Ohr Yisrael,* letter 30.

CHAPTER 36. *Not Taking Joy in Handing Down Rulings*

1. *Bava Batra* 89b.
2. *Sanhedrin* 7a.
3. My expertise in this area had to do with the fact that I wrote a doctoral dissertation in anthropology on Hindu pilgrimage, which meant understanding Hindu temple rites. In the end, the hair from India was not ruled to be a product of idol worship, which coincided with my own view. People have their heads shaved before offering worship as a preparation for devotion, not as part of the ritual itself. Hinduism considers hair and any other bodily part or fluid to be highly polluting, and so one would never offer such a thing in the holy precinct of a temple. In fact, after the hair is removed, the devotee is required to bathe before entering the temple, to restore a state of purity.
4. *Shabbat* 10a.
5. *Ein Ayah,* vol. 4, pp. 52–54.
6. Exodus 23:8.

CHAPTER 37. *Bearing the Burden with the Other*

1. Genesis 40:7.
2. Exodus 3:13–16.
3. *Berachot* 9a, quoted in Rashi, ibid.
4. *Alei Shur* (Jerusalem: Bais HaMussar, 1998), vol. 1, p. 252, and vol. 2, p. 210.

5. Simcha Raz, *A Tzaddik in Our Time* (Jerusalem and New York: Feldheim, 1977).
6. Dovid Rossoff, "Aryeh Levin: Father of the Jewish Prisoners," *Jewish Magazine,* http://www.jewishmag .com/18mag/levin/levin.htm.
7. Collected as *Chochma U'Mussar.* This story according to Rabbi Shlomo Wolbe.

CHAPTER 38. *Judging Others Favorably*

1. *Shabbat* 127b.
2. Leviticus 19:15; *Shavuot* 30a.
3. Perhaps this is the idea being taught in *Pirkei Avot* 1:6: "Make for yourself a teacher, acquire for yourself a friend, and judge all men favorably." Make yourself a student, be a friend, and always look at the positive in others.
4. *Ethics from Sinai* (Jerusalem and New York: Feldheim, 2002).

CHAPTER 39. *Leading Others to Truth*

1. *Sanhedrin* 64a.
2. *Yevamot* 63a.
3. Jeremiah 9:5.
4. *Shulchan Aruch,* Choshen Mishpat 262:21.
5. English doesn't have a word for this feeling, but German does: *schadenfreude,* pleasure in someone else's misfortune.
6. The English word *blanch* has the same connotation.
7. *Ohr Yisrael,* letter 30.
8. *Alei Shur,* vol. 2, p. 533.

CHAPTER 40. *Leading Others to Peace*

1. See *Avot D'Rabbi Natan* 12:3–4 for the techniques Aharon used to bring peace between people.

2. *Michtav mi'Eliyahu*, vol. 2, p. 107.
3. Rabbi Sacks, "Ki Tavo (5770)—Covenant & Conversation," August 28, 2010, www.rabbisacks.org/covenant-conversation-5770-ki-tavo-covenant-conversation/.

CHAPTER 41. *Being Settled in One's Studies*

1. The Hebrew word *ka'as* means either "anger" or "sorrow," depending on the context, revealing a link between these two emotions that isn't obvious but is there to be explored.
2. Rabbi Dov Katz, *The Mussar Movement,* vol. 1, part 1, pp. 204–5.
3. See Rabbi Shlomo Wolbe, *Alei Shur,* vol. 1, pp. 89–91, for more details of what is meant to happen in the two segments of a Mussar session.

CHAPTER 42. *Asking Pertinent Questions*

1. *Pesachim* 116a.
2. *Bava Kamma* 117a.
3. *Mivchar ha'Peninim,* translated by Abraham Cohen as *Choice of Pearls* (New York: Bloch Publishing, 1925), p. 25.
4. Ibid., p. 33.
5. Donald Sheff, letter to the editor, *New York Times,* January 19, 1988.
6. Quoted in Danah Zohar and Ian Marshall, *SQ: Connecting with Our Spiritual Intelligence* (London: Bloomsbury, 2000), p. 15.
7. *Shabbat* 30b–31a.
8. As Hillel addressed his most annoying questioner in the Talmudic story above; see *Shabbat* 30b–31a.

CHAPTER 43. *Listening and Contributing*

1. This meeting and my learning with Rabbi are described in my earlier book *Climbing Jacob's Ladder* (Boston: Trumpter Books, 2007).
2. Deuteronomy 12:32.
3. *Avodah Zarah* 35b.
4. *Gur Aryeh,* Bereishit 29:11; based on verse 4:15 in *Shir Ha'Shirim* (Song of Songs).
5. Galicia, in the introduction to his *Shev Shmaitza* (New York and Trenton, N.J.: Feldheim, 1945).
6. *Siddur Ha'Gra, sefer Keter Rosh, Hilchot Talmud Torah* 56.
7. *Yoma* 28b.

CHAPTER 44. *Learning in Order to Teach*

1. Deuteronomy 6:7.
2. Chapter 22.
3. *Rosh Hashanah* 23a.
4. Shraga Silverstein, trans., *To Turn the Many to Righteousness* (Jerusalem and New York: Feldheim, 1987), chapter 10.
5. *Eruvin* 54b.
6. *Ta'anit* 7a.
7. Trans. Rabbi Yaakov Feldman (Northvale, N.J. and London: Jason Aronson, 1996), p. xlii.

CHAPTER 45. *Learning in Order to Do*

1. *Madregat Ha'Adam,* chapter 14; adapted from a translation by Rabbi Elyakim Krumbein, *Musar for Moderns* (Jerusalem: Yeshivat Ner Shemu'el, 2002), p. 90.
2. *Lev Eliyahu* (Jerusalem: ha'Va'ad le'Hotsa'at Kitve Maran, 1983), p. 1.

3. Exodus 23:5.
4. *Bava Metzia* 32b.
5. Leviticus 19:18.
6. *Ohr Yisrael,* letter 10.
7. Leviticus 19:18.

CHAPTER 46. *Making One's Teacher Wise*

1. *Ruach Ha'Chaim* to *Avot* (Jerusalem: Tushiyah, 1993), 1:4.
2. Proverbs 27:17.
3. The quotation is Proverbs 3:18.
4. *Ta'anit* 7a.
5. See *Megillah* 15b, *Ta'anit* 7a, *Nazir* 59b, *Chulin* 43b, and other places.
6. *Bava Metzia* 59b.
7. Deuteronomy 30:12.

CHAPTER 47. *Clarifying What One Has Heard*

1. *Bamidar Rabbah* 17:5.
2. 1874–1941; scholar, leader, and teacher in prewar Lithuania.
3. *Alei Shur,* vol. 2. pp. 192–94.
4. *Arachin* 15b.

CHAPTER 48. *Saying Something in the Name of Its Speaker*

1. *Megillah* 15a; *Chulin* 104b; *Niddah* 19b.
2. *Pirkei Avot* 4:15.
3. *Sha'arei Teshuvah.*
4. Deuteronomy 8:17.
5. Deuteronomy 8:18.
6. Based on thoughts of Rabbi Mattisyahu Solomon, *mashgiach* of Yeshivat Bet Medrash Gavoha in Lakewood, New Jersey.

7. *Megillah* 6b.
8. Literally, "and I did not find it," as will be explained shortly.
9. *Path of the Just,* p. 327.
10. A *midrash* interprets failing to quote sources as equivalent to stealing from one who is vulnerable: "Rabbi Shimon bar Yochai said in the name of Rabbi Yitzchak bar Tavla who said in the name of Rabbi Chama Aricha who said in the name of Rabbi Acha who quoted the Tanna Rebbe Chiya: 'Whoever does not say something in the name of its speaker transgresses a commandment, as it says [Proverbs 22:22], "Do not rob the destitute because he is destitute"'" (*Yalkut Shimoni,* Mishlei 960). This *midrash* also gives a sterling demonstration of what quoting from sources looks like.
11. *Tosefta Bava Kama* 7:3.
12. *Yalkut Shimoni,* Mishlei 247.

CONCLUSION: *With Heart in Mind*

1. *Sichos Mussar,* pp. 12–13.
2. In his commentary, he is specifically addressing God's direction to Adam and Eve not to eat from the Tree of Good and Evil, but his idea applies here, as well.

.